A Piece of Her Mind

A Piece of Her Mind

Amy McVay Abbott

ISBN-13: 978-1490400211 (CreateSpace-Assigned)

ISBN-10: 1490400214

Available in print and e-book on Amazon.com.

July 2013

In memory of my mother,

Marilyn McVay,

who always enjoyed a laugh.

TABLE OF CONTENTS

INTRODUCTION

A Piece of Her Mind is a collection of "The Raven Lunatic" newspaper columns from 2009 to 2013.

Why the "Raven Lunatic?"

The word Raven comes from my love of Edgar Allen Poe, and is a nod to my middle name, LeNore—as in *"Quoth the raven, nevermore."*

How does the "lunatic" fit in?

Modern life is ridiculous and complicated and fraught with danger. A little laughter is necessary for survival. I see the levity in the garbage disposal that doesn't work because I threw in a whole lemon.

If you are no longer young, the world often wants to chew you up and spit you out like that disposal. If you don't laugh, you die. I write the ridiculous and the sublime and it keeps me sane.

Treat this book like a bag of Sugar Babies at the movie theatre—a sweet treat until full, and then stow away for another time.

Amy McVay Abbott

The Raven Lunatic

July 2013

CHAPTER ONE

Armageddon in Fat Pants

My husband religiously watches the History Channel, which features several shows about the impending end of the world, apocalypse, and doomsday. Will the end be caused by a comet, or an asteroid? Will there be a nuclear holocaust? Will the premiere of *Gnomeo and Juliet* cause the earth's core to melt?

After recently watching a show about a purported Rosicrucian monument in Georgia—a modern day Stonehenge—we determined our plan if suddenly we knew an asteroid targeted the earth in sixty days.

Here's my list.

1. Drink as much of the "real thing"—Coca-Cola—as I can handle. I'm not talking about that fake Coke made with high fructose corn syrup. When I say the real thing, I mean the real thing made in Mexico with real cane sugar. I grudgingly reduced all soda consumption in 2011. Like Queen Victoria, I am not amused. Giving up sodas is supposed to be good for my health, but it makes me cranky. I keep an "Emergency Coke" in the refrigerator door for dire circumstances, like breaking a fingernail.
2. Throw out all my "thin" pants and wear the most decrepit, ancient, stretchy sweatpants I own, plus my holey "I love Books and Cats" T-shirt. Whether at home or out in public, I'll be sloppy-looking and disheveled.
3. Watch every episode of *I Love Lucy* and laugh my behind off (which by then would be large as a barge from drinking all the real colas.)

4. Buy Girl Scout cookies from everyone who asks me. I usually buy one or two boxes from the first girl who asks. Why not have Thin Mints and Coca-Cola for breakfast? If the end is coming, who cares? Add a chaser of Caramel deLites (also known as Samoas) to that mix and live dangerously.

5. Stop changing the cat box. This is an easily-solved problem. I just stop going downstairs. There is not much I need down there. However, if The End comes as a gigantic storm, I might be upset when our safe place smells like a box of "Old Stinkies" as Dr. Watson once said to Sherlock Holmes in an old black and white film.

6. Buy a classic red 1965 Mustang convertible. This represents a bit of a conundrum because if I do number 1 and number 4 (see above), I will need a crane and a wide load sign to lower my girth in and out of the pony car. (Since I will have cashed in my retirement, I can hire George Clooney to help me in and out of the car. If he can't handle it, I'll add Mikhail Baryshnikov.)

CHAPTER TWO

My Bother

I had no warning. My parents did not bother to tell me of his impending arrival. There were no "sibling" classes. Ann Marie was due on Groundhog's Day and darned if she didn't show up three weeks early. And darned if she wasn't a he.

I awakened and found my grandparents in my parent's bed. My grandmother said, *"You have a baby brother."*

What is that?

I was thirty months old. I could not even say the word "brother," so I called him my baby "bother." That has often seemed appropriate.

My parents and I lived in a small Indiana town in a tiny yellow house where something was always wrong with the clothes dryer.

That was the case the day Bother came home from the hospital. The dryer repairman was there when we pulled into the carport.

Dad drove the 1957 pink Chevy he'd bought the day I was born. I huddled next to him on the front seat while Mom held the baby in the back seat. In 1960, car seats and seat belts were still in the future.

When we arrived home, Dad grabbed me by the hand and ran inside the house to see Mr. Vanderipe, the repairman with the funny name.

Did Dad forget something?

The petite young woman had just borne her second child in two-and-a-half years. She needed help getting into the house, on this winter day with the temperature just a few degrees above zero.

Dad never lived that one down. But on that cold day, the dryer was the pressing concern. Weren't there cloth diapers and new baby clothes to be washed and dried?

Things were not going well for me.

It had been weeks since I sat on my mother's lap, and now a skinny varmint of a child took my place.

When Bother was about a week old, life was slowly getting back to normal in the little yellow house. Dad returned to work, teaching high school.

I locked myself in Bother's nursery and beat him over the head with a wooden pop-up toy. This did not play well in Peoria. My mother immediately called my father at school. Classroom teachers weren't often interrupted, especially in the stricter world of 1960. He drove home and took the door off the hinges. The baby screamed, and I sat in my little red chair with my arms crossed in defiance.

This story is now family legend, and I'm often asked of its veracity. I honestly don't remember that day; I was thirty months old. However, I do know that my dad took the wooden pop-up toy, the alleged weapon, back to school with him where it remained until he moved to a new school building in 1971. I was by then a freshman in high school and certainly didn't want or need the pop-up toy.

This incident was the beginning of a long siege with my kid brother that didn't stop until we each had sons, months apart.

This family account offered endless fodder in blaming my brother for sins throughout our childhood. He liked to cite my meanness while I could find every reason to doubt his mental status.

Despite my initial foray into violence, we were pretty normal kids; we could not stand each other.

Though our personalities are alike, we had different interests. He was an outdoor person; I was an indoor person. He liked all animals except cats; I only liked cats.

Our parents embraced seeing "the USA in our Chevrolet." My brother and I often reminisce about fabulous trips of our shared childhood, across Death Valley to Disneyland and Knott's Berry Farm, or up the Blue Ridge Mountains to Monticello and Williamsburg, or down to Florida for Christmas vacation.

My father as both driver and tour guide always got us up so we could get our customary 500 miles on the road. From the proverbial sea to shining sea, we shared good times as a family.

But, every day of every vacation, my brother and I fought over open turf in the back seat.

"Mom, he's on my side."

"She's on my side."

"I'm going to whop you two kids over the head if you don't straighten up right now."

"Whop" is a Hoosier word meaning whack on the head as in *"I whopped my baby brother over the head with a wooden pop-up toy."*

Neither of us ever got whopped, because we always *"straightened up right now."*

Today, my brother and I are close friends. I don't always agree with his politics, and we still have different interests, but we still have a lot of common ground.

We have our moments, especially during political discussions. However, I think I'll keep him.

CHAPTER THREE

Breaking the Ties That Bind

The office supply store overflowed with people. Parents and children loaded up on all the necessary items for a new school year. One could easily identify the college freshman and his nervous parents—Mom clutched a long pre-printed list titled "What to Bring." The father had terror in his eyes, a look that said, *"Some university just cashed the largest check I ever wrote,"* while the prospective freshman had that *"How much longer until I'm away from here"* look.

All this is history for our family.

The trip to sophomore year was much easier than the first trip. Last August the stress in our house was palpable. Our son worried about everything as he prepared to enter college.

We made the two-day trip to his university in a loaded rental van. We got lost several times, despite help from our GPS "Amelia." (Named for Amelia Earhart. *Remember what happened to her?*)

Freshman year, we arrived at our son's new home, an eight-story dormitory. Legions of buxom, scantily-clad sorority girls met us with carts at the front door. Friendly, helpful girls in tiny shorts and halter-tops made nice to my son and husband—then loaded my son's belongings onto carts and helped us to the sixth floor.

No stress. No heavy lifting.

With his own final exams, my college-teaching husband could not go along to pick up our son at the end of the spring semester. I soloed. No chesty helpers this time; the school had cashed our checks by then.

Only one rickety cart was available for all students moving out of this eight-story dormitory. We brought everything down from the sixth floor in elevator loads, but waited 45 minutes for the cart to bring down the heavy TV.

His TV was a tube set with an integrated DVD player. He was thrilled when he received this as a sixteenth birthday gift. He was not as thrilled about this gift when his asthmatic, heavy-breathing, hot-flashing, cranky mother balanced the bulky object on the cart, covered it with garbage bags, and slid haphazardly down the treacherous entrance ramp in the rain to the rented van.

Others in line for the sole cart gazed on us in disregard as we struggled past.

This year his roommate is bringing a 19-inch LCD TV. God bless his roommate.

Freshman year, we arrived just as our son's roommate and parents did. We'd met the roommate and parents earlier in the summer at orientation.

Ever meet someone and felt the vibe that they cannot stand the sight of you? That is the feeling we sensed when we met the roommate's mother at orientation.

The four parents and the matriculates ran into each other several times during orientation. After the initial small talk, the parents seemed to avoid us.

All six of us arrived in Room 621 at exactly the same moment on move-in day. The tiny, square room was jammed with overflowing boxes, electronic gadgets and cords, suitcases, and clothing.

After perfunctory greetings, the roommate's mother said to us, *"I'm very experienced in arranging college dorm rooms as I have two other children at college."*

Okay, then.

My husband and I looked at each other, with that peculiar telepathy long-term married people share: *Get me the heck outta Dodge while there is still time.*

We had not arranged our son's things since he was about six. We did not plan on arranging his college dorm room. Nor was he interested in our comments or our arranging.

We saw that as reasonable parenting.

Our son had a pained look on his face and spent the next two or three hours with his roommate and roommate's parents, the exacting "organized" mother and beleaguered father.

Meanwhile, we went to a museum. Yes, we threw our son under the bus. We came back after the "arranging" was all over.

If an 18-year-old is smart enough to get into college, he can certainly calculate if the microwave/refrigerator combo should be under the cable TV hookup. If your student can't do that by now, there are much graver problems.

How things have changed since I started Old State University in the fall of 1975.

My parents, brother, and I packed the 1973 Impala sedan and drove two hours south from my hometown. I bit my cuticles bloody, probably just as nervous as my own son was on his first trip to college.

I convinced my father that I knew exactly how to get to my dorm. In truth, I did not know anything, and we found ourselves in a subdivision where you could at least see the campus behind a high chain-link fence. An awful moment—as if I was seeing the glittering spires of Oz from inside Folsom Prison—freedom just beyond the fence.

When we finally arrived at my dorm, my room assignment was on the fourth floor. There was no elevator.

My electronic equipment was a wind-up alarm clock, a Smith-Corona electric typewriter, and a Close-n-Play one-piece stereo. No iPod. No television. Not a single lux-u-ry.

Had I owned a television, there was no reception on that side of the building. Indianapolis, the nearest metropolis, had four television channels, five on a clear day, but my side of the building faced away from the signals. Lucky for me, I was entertained all year by blasts of Aerosmith's "Walk This Way" and "Big Ten Inch Record" from the neighboring boys' dorm.

After unpacking numerous pairs of painter's pants, blue jeans, and T-shirts so the suitcases could return home with my parents, it was time to say goodbye.

My mother cried, and my dad said, *"Marilyn, it's time to get on the road."*

I watched them drive away and then immediately went to the basement of the dorm and bought a pack of cigarettes. Not knowing anything about smoking, I bought non-filtered Camels. Does every freshman in college do this?

I had just three or four hours to learn smoking, so I could convince my floor-mates that I was as cool as Bette Davis or Joan Crawford in the old movies. Even with my rhinestone cigarette holder, cool was not in the equation. Choking, hacking, vomiting, maybe; but, cool, no.

Many friends, relatives, and neighbors send children off to college every fall for the first time. The separation is not easy on parents. I cried my eyes out through most of *Team of Rivals*, the audio book we bought for the drive home from our son's freshman trip to college. I'm sure I will cry again when we leave him this year. The separation never gets any easier.

CHAPTER FOUR

Feudalee and Bertram

My husband and I love making stuff up. We aren't quite normal. We repeat this nonsense so often that it becomes a part of our story. Soon, we are not even sure if it is not true.

Take this morning, a perfectly agreeable Saturday morning. We slept in, a lovely bonus sleep time with no alarm clock. The cat slept between us, and it was just chilly enough to enjoy a crumpled blanket over my face.

From next door, the house my husband calls "The Old Thompson Place" we heard much noise, and I got out of bed to investigate. Someone was moving in.

How disrespectful at this hour, the early side of 10 a.m.? Who moves into a house at such an ungodly hour on a Saturday morning?

There was a colossal U-Haul parked in the driveway next to one of those shipping containers MSNBC pundit Ed Schulz points at in his "Lean Forward" commercial. Strangers wandered in and out of the house.

My first thought was so unselfish.

"Where will we park our cars next week when our driveway gets resurfaced?"

My heart filled with love and a welcoming grace towards our new neighbors.

My husband—also filled with the spirit of the Welcome Wagon—and I discussed potential rules and regulations for our new neighbors, who dared to wake us up.

How will we share these rules with them? Perhaps a cake with a note cooked inside, wrapped in foil? Maybe I'll wear a tin-foil hat when I deliver the list.

1. No irritating yappy dogs. Or if they have a dog, it must be mute and able to use a cat box.

2. No children. If they have children, they must be perennially eleven years old and fluent in Suzuki violin, preferably Brahms. Absolutely no drums or large horns.

3. The new neighbors must provide lawn care on our schedule. The neighbors must never mow more often than every ten days, and only between 4 and 5 p.m. on Mondays when we are not home. The prior resident used an extremely large tractor with headlights and mowed night or day, summer, winter or fall. He once mowed on Christmas Eve.

After we established the rules, my husband suggested that I take over *"a nice hot oven meal."* We both laughed uproariously at that one. He's quite the joker!

It was still early, only eleven now, so we went out for breakfast. Still grumpy from the early awakening, I was a little hostile that morning. As we left home I was yelling at my husband over some real or imagined slight. Trying to make me laugh, he started talking in a strange accent as if he imitated our new neighbors.

"Why, looka there. She's yailin at him," my husband said, pretending he was our new neighbor.

I have no idea why he felt our new neighbors talked like extras from *Deliverance* or just walked out of Harper Lee's home church in Alabama, but that's what he said and how he said it.

I decided to play along. Our new neighbors needed names, names we gave them. If we were going to befriend them with a hot oven meal and our foil wrapped note of rules, they needed names.

"Feudalee," I said, for the wife. *"She was named after her great-grandfather, Confederate General Feudal Lee Brown."*

"Bertram for the man," my husband said.

We laughed about that as he backed the car out of the garage. Recovering from our laughter, we realized one bitter truth. We had new neighbors, and they might expect us to speak to them.

CHAPTER FIVE

Secrets of the Hot Oven Meal

Since our son left the nest, I am the chief cook. My husband was the primary cook since early in our marriage, when he was a graduate student; I had a full-time job. Now I have more time, and I am charged with preparing meals (or deciding where we are going to dine).

I do not have a good reputation as a cook, despite winning many white ribbons as an active member of the Go-Getters 4-H Club. My parents recall my setting fire to their pristine kitchen while baking brownies during Food I activities. We had been in our new home less than a year.

Cooking wasn't my strong point. My husband married me for my combination of Jayne Mansfield sex-kitten image, Madame Curie intellect and Phyllis Diller wit.

Tonight I made lasagna that I had prepared dozens of times by following the recipe on the box. Somehow, I neglected to buy the "no bake" noodles and thus made a new family favorite: Crunchy Lasagna. Note: Lasagna should not crackle when chewed.

With my depth of culinary skills, I will now share some family favorites as well as unparalleled cooking tips. Feel free to adjust.

Preparing Vulcanized Tuna Casserole

My husband and I lived in a co-ed dorm in college in the late 1970s. I decided to make Tuna Helper using the dorm's community Radar Range. Prior to the Peloponnesian War, college students did not own their own microwaves.

The "helper" was too soggy, so I added a sleeve of soda crackers, which gave the dish a consistency of baked rubber bands. We had quite a few leftovers from that fiasco.

Strike one.

Handling Germ-Free Chicken Jeanette

This is a·legitimate Florida old-timer recipe containing chicken, various creamed soups, mayonnaise, celery, pimentos, baked with a crust of potato chips and cheddar cheese. I am not kidding about the crust of potato chips and cheddar cheese. I really mean it.

Seyfert's Chips are the best, though Charles' Chips or Ruffles will suffice. On a totally unrelated tangent, this recipe is named for an aged woman whose main claim to fame was that she had never taken off her wedding rings in 60 years. This still turns my stomach. Becauase of this, I always thoroughly clean my hands when cooking sans wedding rings, especially when making a casserole.

I used to make Chicken Jeanette frequently. With the intestinal fortitude of youth, we liked it. Now, I am not so fond of it and haven't yet discovered the Paleo or low carbs version. Chicken Jeanette is probably illegal in most countries, and in this country should not cross state lines due to the toxicity. I am fairly certain it is regulated by the Environmental Protection Agency.

Strike two.

Saran Wrap Does Not Add Flavor

My husband became our primary cook around the time I learned that you do not cover a casserole with Saran Wrap and bake it in the oven, though it does work as a chemistry experiment. How did I learn this: the hard way!

We had moved from Florida to Indiana, and I made a nice casserole in our new townhouse kitchen. As I took it out of the oven, I noticed it had a shiny surface. Even I knew casseroles aren't supposed to shine when they come out of the oven.

"What is that," my husband asked?

The Saran Wrap was baked right into the casserole. We ordered a Domino's pizza that night.

This is what we refer to as "The Incident."

Strike three.

Bonus: Yeasty cinammon rolls with shards of metal

Another culinary faux pas involved the time I baked cinnamon rolls that come in a tin for my family. My intent was for the rolls to be an early Sunday morning surprise. Was my family surprised when my husband found a round, sharp-edged metal lid attached to his roll? My son is a Boy Scout, so my husband's mouth only bled briefly after my son applied his first-aid skills.

Bon appetite.

CHAPTER SIX

A Study of Chin Hair

In a recent scientific study that examined post-menopausal women, researchers determined a causal relationship between the appearance of unsightly, gray chin hairs, their removal, and early onset memory loss.

Leading researchers studied post-menopausal women who—upon discovering this growth, typically ten minutes before a family wedding or photo session—pluck the curly little devils out with raw, unbridled force.

This violent action, researchers postulate, causes two or three uglier, gray hairs to immediately sprout from said chin, and is the first step down a slippery slope to total mental deterioration.

For whom does the bell toll?

Old woman—it tolls for thee. Is your uterus simply dried up or in a specimen jar at Sister Bertrille's Hospital and Home for Aging Baby Boomers?

Indeed, it tolls for thee.

Scientists know the average fifty-four-year old male holds more estrogen in his pinky toe than your average fifty-four-year old female has in her whole body.

Who are these scientists? I have no earthly idea. I'm a writer, not a research scientist. And I'm making most of this crap up.

No wonder old men cry during *Brian's Song* and Folger's coffee commercials.

Clinical researchers deemed this story relevant. It should be shared with the community and women of a certain age for whom that Bad Moon no longer rises.

One clinical subject, whose name we cannot release due to strict confidentiality laws, is a fifty-something, overweight, Caucasian woman of European extraction, who has had her uterus and ovaries removed surgically.

To the uninitiated. this means she has more testosterone in her body than her Uncle Morty (it works both ways).

Since her surgical hysterectomy the subject has sprouted eyebrows that make her look like Broderick Crawford.

The participant has ceased pretending she is a blond, due to personal finances that couldn't swing the eighty dollars a month for color. She is now blessed with silvery, white wiry hair, much of which is on her chin.

For those who did not receive this hirsute gift or still attempt to hide it with bleach, gray hair has a different texture and is kinky.

Yes, I said kinky.

Make of it what you will.

Every two or three days our subject fights a battle with chin hairs. She plucks them out and usually two more grow in within minutes. If she did not pluck them out, she fears she would look like the Warner Bros. cartoon character Witch Hazel.

The study's abstract noted that researchers followed our subject on a typical Friday night to a Chinese restaurant, strictly for observational purposes. Is there a connection between chin hair growth and senior moments? Researchers wanted to know.

The subject had three chin hairs appear that day. Distressed over this development, she was unable to cook dinner and picked up take-out Hunan Chicken. In the restaurant, the subject encountered a familiar face with a toddler on her hip. The mother said to the child, *"Tell Mrs. So-and-So hello,"* and the child said, *"Hello, Mrs. So-and-So."*

The mother's name rattled through our subject's memory bank and came up clueless.

Who was this child's mother?

The face was familiar, but our subject could not place it. Faking familiarity, she patted the child on the back and said to the woman, *"Oh, I've written a book, would you like one of my bookmarks?"*

The child's mother said, *"Well, of course I know you have written a book, silly. You brought a signed copy to my house."*

This narrowed it down quite a bit.

Researchers call this a "conversation stopper." Technically, our subject seems to be lacking in "cognitive function."

Our subject's chin hairs naturally tangled her brain synapses, affecting the scope of recognition and executive function. Language was the next to go, and our subject simply smiled at the child's mother, at a loss for words.

As soon as the mother and child left, our subject asked the guy at the take-out counter who they were. The take-out person knew their names.

Our subject slapped herself on both sides of her head.

"Of course! I know both her children's names and birthdays; I know her father, grandfather, husband and his entire family. They

attend my church. I've been to their house. What in the world is wrong with me?"

Researchers have published this paper and accompanying anecdote to remind all women of a certain age not to pluck, touch, disturb, or tease the chin hairs. Look in the mirror—it may not be too late for you.

CHAPTER SEVEN

Preserving My Rights

I accidentally ate a pickle. My family and close friends know with certainty I never will eat a pickle on purpose. Ever.

At the "have it your way" place, I ordered my burger with ketchup, mustard, onion, lettuce, and tomato.

I punctuated my order with the edict, *"absolutely no pickle."* The clerk must have heard "add more pickle."

Arriving home, I opened my burger and took a generous bite.

Ugh.

Between the buns was a scrawny burger, ketchup, mustard, onion, lettuce, tomato, and six pickles. Six. I counted the heinous, evil, slimy pieces.

I am scowling, thinking about the taste and texture of the vile poisonous pickles.

I brushed my teeth four times.

Pickles are wayward cucumbers. I cannot say enough hurtful things about pickles. However, I will try.

They are disgusting, slippery, spiteful little sticks of green that ruin my life.

One local restaurant serves all its sandwiches with a pickle attached by an American flag toothpick. Attaching a pickle to the symbol of our democracy is defacing our flag, in my opinion. I now give these patriotic pickles—American flag and all—to my husband who relishes them.

The pickle transfer is quick—I do not know what would happen to me should pickle juice touch my sandwich. Instantaneous death?

Let us consider the noble cucumber, freshly picked from an Indiana garden. The Latin name is *Cucumis sativus*, which roughly translated means not fit to cure or can.

Does anything taste as good on a salad or sandwich as a fresh slice of cucumber? That is, of course, rhetorical. A Hoosier Big Boy tomato may be just as good.

Neighbors shared their bounty of cucumbers with us this summer. I've made cucumber salad with Italian dressing, and we've added thin cucumber slices to quarter-pound burgers from the grill.

Sadly, cucumbers often fall astray, into a sour and bitter world for which there is no escape. They lose their fresh appeal and sink into the brine. For this, there is no cure.

My problem with pickles began as a child. In the 1960s television situation comedy *The Andy Griffith Show*. Aunt Bea canned homemade pickles for Andy and Barney.

To preserve her feelings, Andy and Barney praised her "kerosene cucumbers." Aunt Bea entered her canned pickles in the county fair. She lost for the umpteenth time to her rival Clara Edwards (who was also called Clara Johnson for *The Andy Griffith Show* purists who also have no life.)

It just was not kosher.

CHAPTER EIGHT

Philly Flash

On the classic *I Love Lucy Show*, cousin Tennessee Ernie Ford visited the Ricardos from the rural Tennessee town of Bent Fork. Cousin Ernie told Lucy he was *"afeared of wicked city women."*

I am not a convincing wicked city woman. When visiting a city, I gawk up and around like the most stereotypical rube in literature. Pin a sign on me that says, *"Hey, I'm from Indiana—steal my money! And I will make it easy on you by casually ignoring my purse."*

Twenty-five years ago I was visiting New York City with a friend who is accustomed to city life. She admonished me to stop looking up, and more important, stop looking <u>at</u> people. I didn't listen to her and saw Dan Aykroyd on West 57th Street. A *Ghostbuster!*

Years ago, my husband and I visited another college friend who lived in Chicago. She suggested we walk to a certain attraction.

"How far is it," I asked.

"Only seven blocks," she said.

What we clodhoppers from down in southern Indiana did not understand was that ten city blocks make up a larger block. We walked seven miles.

I visited a college friend in Philadelphia recently. She is single and lives in a Deluxe Apartment in the Sky, complete with a doorman, a spa, ground-floor Starbucks, and remarkable access to culture and the accoutrements of the city. I love visiting her life. It is quite different from my suburban/semi-rural life.

But, I'm too inflexible for the city life. *Green Acres is the place for me!* For one thing, what my city dwellers consider "a few blocks" for a walk is like marathon training for me.

My Philadelphia friend is a good host. We visited an excellent art museum one day and saw treasures by Renoir, Monet, and the local boys, Eakins and Wyeth. After the dip into culture, my friend suggested we take a tourist trolley to check out historic sites on the return home.

The non-English speaking trolley driver seemed a little erratic and the trolley itself lacked brakes and shocks. The seats were well-worn wooden benches. We left the Philadelphia Museum of Art on this balmy spring day, boarding the trolley in a happy and relaxed state. Within minutes, I felt as Jim Carrey in *The Mask* had hijacked us on the whirlwind trip through Fairmount Park. Very quickly and zipping by, we also saw:

- Rowers in skulls on Schuylkill River, zip.

- Benjamin Franklin Free Library, zip.

- Front of art museum and Rocky sculpture, zip.

- Robert Indiana LOVE monument, zip.

We were sitting on the back row of the trolley. As the wandering driver rounded a corner, I slid all the way across the row and slammed into my friend.

Zip.

My friend suggested we visit Franklin Fountain, a charming ice cream place we had visited last summer on another of my repeated visits. This was a splendid idea and a perfect ending to a lovely afternoon. The map indicated the trolley stopped at Second and Market, near the ice cream place.

We flew up Market Street in rush hour traffic, weaving wildly around City Hall. Did the statue of William Penn atop City Hall wag a finger, shocked at the speed of the trolley?

For a little-trolley-that-could, the driver certainly held his own with errant taxi drivers and speedy lawyers in black SUVs racing home to the suburbs.

Zip.

We missed a few stops. Okay, no big deal.

"Was that the Liberty Bell off to the left?"

"Did we just see Independence Hall, now somewhere in a fog behind us?"

Zip.

Counting down the streets now, we approached the stop. Apparently, the driver had not read the map as we whipped past Second and Market around the ice cream shop.

My friend walked to the front of the trolley, swinging her arms from one handhold to the next to keep her balance. The driver yelled at her in an unknown island dialect, loudly.

To heck with her politeness: I screamed, *"Hey, driver, did you miss Second and Market?"*

He ignored us.

By now, we had crossed I-95 and were on a remote trolley island, hanging over the Delaware River. The driver finally stopped the trolley and continued yelling at my friend.

We figured this was the end of the line, another thirty yards and we would be in the river. How did we end up here, halfway to Camden, New Jersey? How do we get back to the Old City?

31

For my friend, the consummate city dweller, it was not a long walk. For me—who sometimes drives to my mailbox—I wasn't sure I was up to it after a long day. My lumbar spine was hammered like a piece in a Jenga game.

A supervisor got on the bus and explained that the Philly Flash bus season had just opened last weekend. Some new drivers *"didn't quite get it yet,"* explained the supervisor. Apparently the new driver thought he was driving a city bus and paid no attention to the pre-determined stops. Even country folk like me know the difference between a city bus and a trolley.

The supervisor directed us to her bus and took us to Third and Market, just a block from our destination.

At last. Franklin Fountain and a chocolate malted made the old-fashioned way, in a large, metal cup, lumps of cold vanilla ice cream, milk, and malted crystallizing on my spoon. This Wicked City Woman surely enjoyed that pleasure of the flesh in the Big City.

CHAPTER NINE

The Mad Dash for Eggs

Since forever, the Lions Club in my little hometown has hosted an Easter egg hunt. The Lions Club is a strange bunch, err, Pride, with eccentric fraternal rituals.

My father—who once held an group office called the Tail-Twister—sometimes returned from meetings with his tie cut in half. He had been "fined" for something as silly as his beloved Chicago Cubs winning a game. Dad and the other members often paid the price for sins real or imagined. Fines and fundraisers enabled the club to raise money for their various charities and host the annual Easter egg hunt.

My memory book reflects a different time—an era when schoolteachers wore ties and a time when ties were inexpensive enough to slice in half.

On a spring morning in 1965, the wild men of the Lions Club hid multi-colored plastic eggs in the field behind the elementary school.

Several hundred children—these were future Baby Boomers—lined up in age groups, tightly clutching yellow, lavender, and green braided Easter baskets. Anticipation hung over the crowd and parents held children back from the mad dash to find eggs.

The wide-eyed children wondered which eggs held candy and which had coins?

In the crowd, there were the ringers. One family boasted several children and they resembled Amazons in their physical abilities. Each year when the elementary school had a track event, members of this family won almost every event.

Each age group for the Easter egg hunt had one of these children in it. I knew they would immediately find the treasures.

Close family friends of ours were also there with their three beautiful, lean, athletic daughters. Unlike my brother and me, they were the first chosen at Red Rover and the other reindeer games. The family's oldest daughter is a lifelong friend of mine.

Ready. Hundreds of little legs arched forward, baskets in hand.

Set. Hundreds of wide eyes looked out to the field, now carpeted with plastic eggs.

Go. The Lions Tail-Twister shot off his starter pistol and the Amazon children and the family friends lurched forward, leaving me in their wake.

"Go, get the eggs," my parents shouted, chagrined that we were still standing there, in the dust of the other more eager children.

Soon all the childrens' baskets overflowed with the bounty of this Christian holiday. Even my brother had a few eggs in his basket.

Where was I?

Dawdling, like Prissy in *Gone with the Wind.* Looking around and planning my strategy; tying my Keds Red Ball Jets in large, slow loops.

I almost lost my balance as a child with a broken leg breezed past me.

Okay, maybe I should start. I ran my hardest.

I spy a yellow egg with my little eye.

34

Gone, Amazon child number four swoops in and gets my egg. And it has a quarter inside! There, over by the towering maple tree, a blue/green orb. I am off to get it, running, running, running, out of breath. Then it is gone.

Every year it was the same story. Reach for the tissues and weep for me. My sad, sad tale is of the child who is ever beaten at this ritual. Let's see if I can make this story even more pathetic. Imagine I'm dressed in blue plaid pants that are too short, and my mother has insisted on this cold late March day that I wear a hat that makes me look like Elmer Fudd.

Are tears rolling down your cheeks? Do you feel the anguish? Is there pity and pathos for this little wretch who is not unlike a Dickens character?

Flash forward thirty years. Same Lions Club, 1995 version. Same Lions Club members, now they are pepaws, papas and grandpas. Same little village.

The Amazon children have mated with other powerful peoples, and their children populate the town.

Even though I moved away in 1975, I remember and watch them stretching in their athletic clothing like Olympic track stars.

In addition, my friend, the oldest of the beautiful sisters is there with her children. Her daughter, who is a year older than my son, is a beautiful, athletic child.

Did I mention I'm having a serious flashback to 1965?

Ready. Hundreds of jumping legs of the Baby Boomer's children lean forward with their plastic, wire-handled buckets.

Set. Hundreds of hands thrust Game Boys into Thomas the Tank Engine or Barney the Dinosaur jacket pockets and face forward.

Go. Grandpa Tail-Twister fires the starter pistol, and children rush forward and fill buckets with eggs.

My son, who is five, stands at the starting gate and looks around.

Is he supposed to run?

My husband and father are shouting at him, *"An egg. Go over there. Behind the tree. Look in the hole. See the pink plastic egg. It's right there."*

He saunters around the course as some of the athletic children of my school peers fly past him.

He is thinking about something else. Maybe the big Lego tower he built at Grandma's?

My childhood friend stands next to me, smiling and laughing, and not remembering my horror of thirty years ago.

Her daughter runs to her with a purple bucket full of eggs.

Where is my son? He is tumbling in the grass, bucket askew.

Some eggs do not fall far from the chicken.

CHAPTER TEN

Ontogeny Recapitulates Phylogeny

When did I discover that I was a nerd? Husband asked me the other night, moments after I arranged my bed pillows for the umpteenth time in what I refer to as my "pillow system."

Nerds are born not made. Certainly in my case there was a genetic predisposition (I cite as evidence a family snapshot of father, summer 1964, plaid Bermuda shorts, white short-sleeved collared shirt, wing-tips, black socks, plastic pencil protector). I have been nurtured by others of my kind.

I always knew deep within myself. I am a nerd.

There were early signs. How many first graders write with a fountain pen? I did not learn to ride a bike until I was almost nine—and showed no anxiety in having training wheels on a bike with 26-inch wheels. When you are over five feet in the third grade, you get a big bike.

A friend often reminds me of my portable battery-powered fan that I carried in junior high.

While I was not a math or science whiz, I loved gadgets and spent my allowance for a Dymo Label Maker and labeled everything in my parents' kitchen after we moved to our new house.

My mother is not a nerd. She has always been a beautiful and stylish woman, in the Elizabeth Taylor *Father of the Bride* mode. However, she contributed to my nerdiness with a continual, unrelenting need to curl my hair, a series of permanents that neither tamed nor organized my thick, black locks. Mom took me to her beautician Mrs. M, who had

37

orange hair and a house that reeked of cigarette smoke, perm solution, and one wet Chihuahua.

Mom gave up on my hair when I was in the sixth grade. Today I have the same haircut I did in the sixth grade and the same thick-rimmed glasses. At least some things stay the same.

Advice to the pre-teen parent: do not get your child glasses that look like prison-issue. I wanted the popular wire-rimmed glasses, like John Lennon wore.

No daughter of mine is wearing those hippie glasses.

I forgive my parents for these indiscretions, for I have had an abundantly happy life.

What was the source of this happiness? I found another nerd. I know many people feel that our kind should not marry, rather live in civil unions. But nerds deserve legal happiness also. Nerds want the same rights as all Americans.

I met my partner at a college yearbook workshop. He owned a nerd magnet of a car. His mode of transportation was an aged Cadillac that needed a nineteen-cent Bic pen stuck in the carburetor to order to start. Do you think I could go for a guy with a Trans-Am? No way.

We have lived in our nerdy bliss now for 25 years this October. Nothing makes us happier than an evening at Barnes and Noble or a trip to Sam's Club for new reading glasses. We both love our gadgets. Tomorrow I'm getting my husband a new Salad Spinner. Life is good.

CHAPTER ELEVEN

Open Mouth, Insert Foot

I come from a long line of talkers. The more a talker talks, the greater likelihood of a gaffe.

1926. Springfield, Illinois—When my grandfather was a budding sales rep, he walked with a customer on a city street. A hefty woman walked ahead of them—her considerable size visible about a block away.

"That's the fattest woman I've ever seen," my lean, six-foot something grandfather said to his companion and customer.

"That's my sister," the soon-to-be-ex-customer said.

Not knowing exactly what to say, my now horrified grandfather spit out, *"Oh, but I'll bet she is awfully good!"*

And that was the end of that.

1981. Rural Indiana—My cousin saw a friend in the bathroom at a wedding reception.

"Great to see you, when is your baby due?" inquired my curious cousin.

"I'm not pregnant," said the soon-to-be-ex-friend.

And that was the end of that.

1988. Elsewhere in Indiana—Our family shared Christmas dinner, with great food and much laughter. We discussed Christmas traditions.

My father looked at his two grandsons, both age eight, and said, *"When did you boys learn that Santa Claus isn't real?"*

There were some strange looks, and dead silence. Grandpa let the cat out of the bag, and the adults at the table laughed and laughed and laughed.

And that was the end of that.

Yesterday.   Southern Indiana—While calling on a long-standing account, I was curious as to why Melissa was eating chips and salsa at nine in the morning.

I asked her, *"Don't you realize that Cinco de Mayo was over a week ago?"*

She glared at me and began speaking in Spanish, which I will loosely translate, *"You are an idiot. Cinco de Mayo is a made-up American holiday, and the real Mexican Independence Day is celebrated in the fall."*

And that was the end of that.

The lesson I continue to learn—over and over and over—is think before you open your yapper.

And that is the end of that.

CHAPTER TWELVE

Feline Feces Management 101

With our son off at college, the ritual, weekly changing of litter boxes has fallen to me. Being exceptionally lazy, I greatly dislike this chore. Rather than scoop the evidence, I bought four plastic litter pans from the dollar store. When the pans get too disgusting, I throw them out and buy new ones. (I don't want to hear from all you environmental wacko extremists; at least I get the environmentally friendly litter. Get over it.)

The weekly Changing of the Boxes happens every Sunday night before the trash goes to the curb. (Doesn't that sound as if something magical and wonderful happens, as if the cans lift up and fly to the curb on the wings of an angel?)

Restated: The Changing of the Boxes happens every Sunday night before my sweet husband drags the cans to the curb.

A month ago a tree branch too large for our little chain saw fell on the concrete slab beside our basement door. This is also where the garbage cans are kept. One can was way too heavy to lift or roll around the limb, so it stayed there for a couple of weeks until we had the branch removed.

I left out a minor point here because it involves me, and I don't come out looking all that good.

I was not bagging the cat litter, rather only dumping the odiferous contents into the garbage can. And I had again—in my extreme ennui about anything remotely related to work in any form—neglected to put the lid back on the can of feline feces.

41

Didn't pay much attention; I don't go outside unless there's a fire drill.

With the lid off the trash can our May rainstorms caused the cat poop to set like cement, rendering the plastic trash into an unwielding boulder. My beloved—who has been in physical therapy for a wrenched shoulder for several weeks—heroically moved the can to the curb.

Monday morning came and the can was so immovable that the trash haulers simply left it in the street.

We ignored this—stuffed some garbage bags on top—believing that the next week the garbage men would not remember a heavy, hardened mass of cat manure.

Week two—our garbage men are no fools.

So, the dilemma? What to do?

Plan A: My Lucy Ricardo-inspired solution (and I always have one) was to put the can on a dolly, drag it out behind the yard barn, turn it upside down and semi-bury the lip into the ground and wait for winter.

By then, it would have become an attractive, icy, frozen glob of cat ca-ca. Then it could easily broken up and thrown into the woods where nymphs and fairies would use it as fertilizer in their gardens.

Plan B: We get another broken trash can and replace the one with the cat do-do in it and tape a sign on the outside that says, "Please remove our old garbage can."

I believe in my heart that if it is a good sign—written legibly with a Sharpie and no *Beverly Hillbillies* rudimentary printing—this will convince the garbage men to take it away.

Our neighbor's house went up for sale last week, and I am sure they are enchanted as the sensory delights waft upstream to their home.

Monday is only a few days away. Will the garbage men haul away the giant poopsicle? Stay tuned.

CHAPTER THIRTEEN

Garbage In—Garbage Out

My husband worked four nights in a row and now has a day off. I wanted to make a nice dinner for him tonight as I was gone for the past three days and he eating God-knows-what.

I crept out of our bedroom soundlessly around seven a.m. and took the cat with me. The gray, furry animal likes to wake up my husband by putting his cold, wet nose on my husband's warm, dry one.

In the quiet kitchen, I browned some lean stew meat, peeled sweet potatoes and chopped an onion. I minced garlic cloves and added the entire mixture to the Crock-Pot along with a bay leaf, a cinnamon stick, tomatoes and a pinch of allspice. Eight hours later, I added apricots and fresh parsley for a delicious winter stew.

There's a prequel to this domestic bliss. A week ago, I dropped a rotting lemon in the garbage disposal, failing to cut the lemon in pieces. Rookie mistake.

This morning, after I concocted my stew, I turned on the cold water and started pushing the sweet potato peelings into the garbage disposal.

No satisfying grinding noise, no tearing the peels to pieces. There was a dull roar as the motor tried as hard as it could. I think I can. I think I can, said the little garbage disposal that couldn't.

The water in the sink started to spin counter-clockwise and slosh over the sides.

My husband came into the kitchen in his "Rock 'em Sock 'em" retro T-shirt and Stewie from "Family Guy" pajama bottoms.

He's a keeper!

He rubbed the sleep out of his eyes and came over to the sink and said, *"Well, it worked fine this weekend while you were gone."*

With a large flashlight, he crawled underneath the sink and completed the due diligence that all husbands do in times of mechanical crisis. Press this button. Tighten this bolt. Shake it all about.

As sexist as this sounds, I have observed this behavior in men repeatedly. Husbands want wives to think they know what they are doing.

Often they don't. Why shouldn't I screw up the garbage disposal at least once in a nearly three-decade marriage? Who's with me on this? I would say he owes me one....

Flashback 1991. On a pleasant Sunday afternoon, I took the baby to the mall. All was peaceful and well in our little house when I left and all was peaceful and well when I returned.

As I pulled into the driveway, Terry the Plumber was leaving in his truck. I thought, *"Why is Terry here on a Sunday? That's really strange."*

When we went into the house, my husband was watching football in the family room just as he was when we left.

One small incident happened while we shopped.

My husband learned the hard way you don't plunge the garbage disposal when it is clogged.

Terry came out and installed a new disposal at Sunday rates.

Terry has since gone to that great plumbing business in the sky, but our latest local plumber will be available between twelve and two to undo my damage.

CHAPTER FOURTEEN

The Agony of Getting to the Ecstasy

The destination is the ecstasy—either the smooth marble temple or the legendary spires on ancient, fragile treasures or the craggy mountain and the red rocks or the white-pebbled, frothy shoreline.

The travel is the agony—either the subway car where someone drippy sneezes directly on you or the cab ride to the airport in a "Cash for Clunkers" with no shocks. What about the pat-down at the TSA security line at the airport after you sorted your life in four large gray bins (laptop, shoes, purse, cell phone and charger, 3-ounce bottle of Visine, bifocals, jacket, umbrella, and carry-on bag, the one with "I'm a Tourist from Indiana, Rob Me" printed on the side.)

Last weekend we flew back from an east coast city, grateful that returning to southern Indiana involved only one connecting stop. The first leg of the trip was uneventful and on a standard-sized jet.

Only when we arrived at the connecting airport did the complete agony fully reveal itself.

About thirty minutes before the thirty- minute flight, the informative gate attendant began making announcements.

Welcome to Regional Midwest International Airlines. We are glad that you are flying with us today.

We board by zones. Please remain in your seat until your zone is called and then you may come through the gate.

First, I want to welcome persons who need special assistance, parents with small children, and elderly people or those in wheelchairs may board.

The gate monitor continued:

Next, we want to welcome our frequent fliers, members of our Special Club, members of our Really Special Club, Civil War generals, business class passengers, goat herders, goats, and those with a pentagram stamped on their ticket. This group may use our special "breezeway" and bypass me at the gate.

About two-thirds of the group got up and went through the "breezeway." We do not fly often enough to make collecting frequent flier points or joining the special upgrade clubs worthwhile.

This breezeway idea made absolutely no sense to me. The small plane could not hold more than forty-five people. We were all headed down the same jetway, outside to a shaky metal set of stairs, around on the concrete tarmac to the plane, and up its small fold-out stairs.

What is special about an imaginary eight-foot "breezeway" marked off by theatre ropes?

Who buys a business class ticket to walk through a rope line?

Attention, passengers. Now we are ready to board zones one and two.

About ten remaining passengers stood up and presented their crumpled paper tickets.

The gate clerk pointed to us, the two remaining, and said,

Finally, zone three, you, that couple in the corner wearing bifocals and looking like you were chosen last for Red Rover on the elementary school playground.

Yes, You two, Zone Three, come ahead.

Sheepishly, we went through the gate, ashamed that we did not belong to the Real Special Club or herd goats.

Now we were all on the plane, and ready to take off. The flight attendant gave a lengthy oration.

Blah, blah, blah, just like the never-seen teacher in Charlie Brown cartoons.

Please do not sit in an exit row if you are under fifteen years old, easily distracted, or think that you will block the exit.

I did not hear much of her speech, distracted by shiny things on the cover of "Sky Mall" magazine.

The uneventful flight took about 28 minutes and we were on the ground at home, vowing to sign up for the upgrade next time.

CHAPTER FIFTEEN

Groundhogs, Raccoons, and Other Inconsiderate Critters

When I was a child, my parents read my brother and me stories from the book *Little Brown Bear Goes to School*. A simplistic story about animals on a picnic, the book featured Miss Ringy Raccoon, a prim and proper schoolteacher.

I loved this book, but I do not love encounters with wild or domestic animals, like the overly enthusiastic German shepherd who stalks me every time I visit my mailbox. Members of my family farmed for generations. Apparently, I did not get the animal-loving gene.

Three years ago on Mother's Day, my husband awakened me.

"Honey, there's more than one mother on the property today."

At the kitchen window, we saw Mother Groundhog, Father Groundhog, and four baby Groundhogs. (Mrs. Groundhog is the varmint version of "Octomom" because groundhogs do not usually have quadruplets, but more often twins.)

We called in a critter removal company. One by one, trap by trap, the groundhog family relocated to a Groundhog Witness Protection program in Kentucky. The critter technician explained that animals such as groundhogs need relocated several miles away, or they will return to this habitat.

I doubted that these critters really were going away. In my imagination, I pictured the critter truck driving just out of sight and releasing all six of the brown monsters. I'm just cynical that way.

While watching television on a Friday evening, we heard loud noises above the master bedroom closet. The noises moved, scurrying loudly around the house above our son's bedroom, my office, and the bathroom. The frantic scampering continued Saturday Sunday night.

Same time. Same station. Same raccoon channel.

For three evenings, I was a prisoner of my home, broom in hand, banging on the ceiling wherever the offending creature made his presence known. The critter man charges triple time on a weekend; we waited until Monday to call him.

My husband asked me to stop banging on the ceiling for fear of making holes. Strictly following his wishes, I banged on the walls, which frightened and tormented our befuddled cat.

Why do things like this always happen after five p.m. on Friday?

Thank you, Mr. Murphy and your stupid, immutable law.

With the help of a home inspector who is also a friend, we secured a Varmint Catcher (V.C.) who came on Tuesday afternoon.

Said V.C. went up into the attic and came down quickly, noting at least one varmint, most likely a raccoon, spending evenings with us. The debris left behind indicated that it had merely been a short visit.

The Varmint Catcher found two holes in the soffit on either end of the house. He'll fix them after the varmint retreats or is captured. He'll set a trap (with cat food as bait) on the roof of the house near one of the holes.

V.C. educated us about raccoons. This is their mating season; if he catches a female, he will re-bait the trap. He said where there is a female there is a male. Ah, young love.

Baby raccoons do not normally arrive until late spring, so if the Beast is a she, she is probably just scouting for a new home. The V.C. also said raccoons have a four-to-five-mile range, so she may have several bed and breakfasts in the neighborhood.

I mentioned to my husband that I hoped to take a picture of the trapped creature. He said, *"That would be good. Then you can at least document that you aren't just a crazy middle-aged woman who thinks she has animals in her attic."*

Now we wait. The trap is on the roof and we are vigilant. A night has passed and all was quiet on the attic front. My broom stands ready in the corner near the bed.

Has the varmint moved on to another location? Did the smell of the human in the attic drive her away? Is she on spring break in Daytona?

CHAPTER SIXTEEN

In the Land of the Lost

The heat index was a balmy 120 degrees, with air so thick it hung from the clouds in chunks. The middle-aged married couple shopped for stone statuary for their new rock garden.

She wanted a three-foot concrete Sinclair dinosaur among other things—perhaps a concrete turtle, or a pineapple, or a sundial? Maybe a bird bath? Who doesn't want to display heavy, tasteless concrete animals in their yard?

The couple drove to the statuary store in another county. She found the best turtle, one with a small stone head popping up, perfect for the garden. The store had no dinosaurs. Purchasing Dino would come on another day.

But, on this hot Saturday, with the trunk of the couple's sedan weighed down with stone statuary, the couple wanted lunch.

The town with the concrete store covered less than a square mile and had a population of about 1,000 people, but reportedly had a fantastic Thai place. Here's how it went.

Her: *Turn right, then turn left.*

Him: *Do you mean turn left?*

Her: *No, you can't turn left; it is a dual lane highway. Turn right and then turn left right there.*

Him: *Do you mean turn around?*

Her: *Yes, turn right when you leave the driveway—get in the left lane, and then turn back on the other side.*

Him: *Where's the restaurant?*

Her: *I looked on the Google map before we left and I know right where it is. The map said it was on Coal Mine Road down from Sandy's Pizza. Okay, go up to this light and turn right.*

Him: *Do you mean here? There are lots of roads around here named Coal Mine Road.*

Her: *Yes, I mean here, turn right NOW.*

Him: *Now when? I don't see anything that vaguely resembles a business.*

Her: *Well, I can't remember the cross street but I think it is Gibson. Yeah, it's at the corner of Coal Mine and Gibson past the school.*

Him: *Well, we've driven past the school and there's no sign and no Gibson Street.*

Her: *Okay, turn right and we'll try to find Sandy's Pizza.*

Him: *How does finding Sandy's Pizza help us find the Thai place?*

Her: *Well, I kind of know where it is on the map so if I see Sandy's Pizza I'll know where we are.*

Him: *That makes no sense whatsoever.*

Her: *Look, there's Sandy's Pizza.*

Him: *Great, now what do we know?*

Her: *Nothing, I guess I was wrong. Let's go downtown and see if we can find somebody to ask.*

Him: *This town is too small to have a downtown and I'm turning around.*

Her: *Oh, please just go this way. I know there's a downtown. I was here ten years ago.*

Him: *Okay.*

Her: *Hey, let's ask this lady over there.* (He pulls over where an elderly lady bends over in her garden, wearing an oversized white floppy hat and blue pedal pushers, and strangely resembling painted wooden cutouts of a woman's oversized behind so popular in rural America.)

Him: *You ask her! I'm not going to ask her.*

Her: *Ma'am, where is the Thai restaurant?*

Wooden Cutout Lady: *Well, this lady runs it out of her house and it's on Coal Mine road on the north side of the road. If you want I'll go inside and get my phone book.*

Her: *No, that's okay; we'll find it.*

Him: *Okay, now how does that help us?*

Her: *Dang, I wish I still had my smart phone and we could Google it.*

Him: *I wish we had brought the GPS. Okay, now, I'm going back to Coal Mine Road and drive back up to the school.*

Her: *Okay, I think I saw it. Hey, you passed it. Slow down, I think you missed it.* (He turns car around in the school parking lot.)

Him: *Where in the heck IS this place?*

Her: *Turn right now, TURN RIGHT here. Why did you pass it?*

Him: *It doesn't look like there is anything back there. I'm going around the back and see if I can get there from the back.*

Her: *But I saw a sign, you missed the sign.*

He drives around the block and into the driveway.

Him: *Where's the sign?*

Her: *Well, I thought I saw a sign. Hey, let's ask this guy.* (Man standing by truck next to building where there was allegedly a sign five minutes earlier.)

Him: *No, I am not stopping. Three strikes and you are out!*

Her: *Well, where are we gonna do?*

Him: *I'm driving over the railroad tracks on Coal Mine Road. It has to be over the tracks.*

Her: *No way, I'm sure it isn't over the tracks. How could it be over the tracks?*

He drives over the tracks and points to the sign that says "Thai Chou."

Her: *Look, there's the Thai place.*

Upon arrival, he had stir-fry shrimp and she had crow.

CHAPTER SEVENTEEN

Don't think about Baseball

Bear with me; this is indeed a story about baseball. I round the bases before I get to home plate.

Last night, I needed to water some new shrubs. The landscapers rolled the hose back into the reel, which sits on a rock bed adjacent to the house. I went out the back door in ancient, floppy pink house shoes, expecting to turn on the faucet for the sprinklers.

Instead, I unrolled the hose into the yard and arranged it so the water would hit both the new lilac bushes and budding grass. I ran back across the prickly straw over the new grass and turned the water on as sharp rocks poked through the bottoms of my worn slippers.

I stood back to assess where the water was going. It wasn't even close.

Rather than walk on the rock bed again, I ran out under the sprinkler and moved it. I reassessed.

Without my glasses on, I wasn't even getting close.

After three attempts, I got it right, but was soaked from head to toe.

Dripping water, soaked to the bone, I went back into the house. I passed my husband who was watching a baseball game, and I headed upstairs to dry off and change clothes.

I returned to the basement and my husband said, *"Oh, did you just take a shower?"*

What is the point of this story? This is a story about baseball.

My husband did not see me go outside; he missed the entire water drama. He didn't notice my passing him, dripping like Niagara Falls and leaving a water trail.

Why? It's because the Cincinnati Reds now broadcast in High Def. I know you are as excited about this mesmerizing social development as I am.

Now I can see the sweat on Jay Bruce's brow.

I was born to a Cubs fan, married a Reds fan (still National League) and now my son is courting a girl who is a Red Sox fan. (I know, American League. As I write these words, their Saturday night date is a Nationals/Mets game.)

Last Sunday I spent the day with my mother so my father, brother, husband, and nephew could go to Wrigley Field. Perhaps you've heard of it? It's a baseball stadium north of the Chicago Art Institute and the other great treasures of culture in the Second City.

The men in my life really like baseball.

I've been in more major league baseball parks than most people. I saw Denny McClain pitch in old Tiger Stadium; I sat across from the "Green Monster" in Fenway, and I've stood on home plate in San Francisco. I saw Rafael Palmero hit a few out of the park at Arlington, Texas, and I witnessed Bo Jackson's first White Sox at-bat, when he smacked a home run out of old Comiskey on a cold April Opening Day.

I've attended many games in Cincinnati and Chicago. We were there on Opening Day at old Riverfront Stadium when former Reds' owner Marge Schott hosted a parade, including a large elephant onto the field.

But here's the problem. I don't give a Wiffle ball about baseball. I've pretended to like it for more than half a century, long enough to understand fundamental baseball words like "change-up" and "tater."

I don't tolerate heat well, and so for every stadium I've listed I also learned where it's first-aid station is located. That's where they keep the free "cool" packs.

On my fortieth birthday I drank one cold beer on that hot July day and threw up for twelve hours. Rather than leave the park, my family of eight moved from third-base seats at Riverfront to the shaded patio above the outfield.

We could not leave the game, for heaven's sake; it was the Cubs versus the hometown Reds.

That was the same game where my dad put the mail-order tickets in his bank's lock-box and it nearly took an Act of Congress getting re-issued tickets. Then, before game day, he remembered where they were.

I'm as done with baseball as I am with rock concerts, short dresses, and four-inch heels.

I watch the odd game sitting next to my husband, tossing out periodic appropriate remarks.

"Did you see Scott Rolen hit that tater?"

I live in southwestern Indiana where the "red bird" isn't the Indiana state bird, it is a Cardinal as in St. Louis Cardinals—Stan Musial, Whitey Herzog, and some fellah named Albert Pujols.

Over the years, I have learned a few things about baseball. Like why did the manager leave Cubs' pitcher Rick Sutcliffe in so long during the 1984 playoffs?

Who in the world likes the designated hitter rule? I mean, come on.

And what about Texas Ranger Josh Hamilton whose Windex-blue eyes are so translucent that his daytime average is a miserable .111— yet, he can pop those home runs out at night?

Of note, I need to tell you about the game I did not attend. While in Anaheim, California my brother and father attended an Angels' game and saw the legendary Nolan Ryan pitch, while mom and I stayed at the hotel and watched a rerun of *The Flip Wilson Show*. My brother loves telling his brush-with-greatness-story. I was fine in the cool hotel room, watching Geraldine.

CHAPTER EIGHTEEN

Customer Service

Tonight I was minding my own business on a Big Box store website and a chat person jumped in. I copied and saved the web chat. Names have been changed to protect the annoying.

Chat: *Welcome to our website. Would you like to chat online with a customer service representative?*

Me: *Sure.*

Chat: *Please wait for a representative to respond. This chat may be monitored or recorded for quality assurance purposes. Your average wait is 53 seconds. Thank you for holding.*

Chat: *You are now chatting with Peggy. How may I help you?*

Me: *We are remodeling our kitchen soon and I want to get my appliances from your store. I am starting to look for refrigerators and I want a moderately sized one with ice cube making capability but not water in the door. Stainless, side by side with freezer on bottom.*

Peggy: *Thank you for contacting Chat! My name is Peggy. May I have your name please?*

Me: *It's Amy.*

Peggy: *Hi, Amy.*

Peggy: *Thank you for choosing our store.com, I will be glad to assist you with the information regarding the refrigerator.*

Amy: *Can you get filtered water for ice cubes in this one?*

Peggy *Amy, do you have any specific brand in mind?*

Amy: *I like X Brand first. After that I am not sure.*

Amy: *Prefer most of it to be made in US.*

Amy: *If that is even possible.*

65

Peggy: *Thank you for the information, Amy.*

Peggy: *May I know the capacity of the side-by-side refrigerator?*

Amy: *25 or so cubic feet.*

Peggy: *Thank you for the information, Amy.*

Peggy: *Please stay on hold for 2-3 minutes while I find this information for you. You may click on the below link to check out today's Deal of the Day item.*

Peggy: *Please click here.*

Amy: *Don't really need an anvil pruner today, Peggy. And I don't need men's boots. But the metric wrench looks pretty interesting. Maybe I can use it on my NEW REFRIGERATOR. (caps indicate screaming.)*

Peggy: *Thank you for your patience, Amy.*

Peggy: *Please click here to see item.*

Peggy: *Please go through the item listed on the above page, I hope you like it.*

Amy: *Okay, well, first I can see that it has a dispenser and I only want ice and it isn't stainless steel. I mentioned both of these things in my first message.*

Peggy: *Thank you for the information, Amy.*

Amy is now clicking back and forth from Facebook, wandering away and losing patience.

Peggy: *Please click here.*

Amy: *Thank you, Peggy. I'll be printing this out and taking it to the store so I can see the item in person.*

CHAPTER NINETEEN

Flouring the Cat

Last Christmas, I learned a secret about some of my neighbors. I am a trusting person, and I had no idea this behind-the-scenes activity existed. I am not talking about the alleged whereabouts and existence of one Jolly Old Elf. This is more nuanced.

Some people actually hire designers to decorate their homes for the holidays. Seriously. I'm naïve, but I had no idea.

I learned this when researching and writing a magazine story about Christmas decorations in our community. Those who use a professional decorator want their secret kept. So I won't name names, but you know who you are.

To each her own, but part of our holiday joy involves certain peculiar and random traditions. We prefer the old-fashioned way, an eclectic mix of decorations and gifts gathered from our personal experiences. All our holiday paraphernalia is kept in plastic storage tubs.

As our family grew, we obtained more holiday decorations, which meant getting more storage tubs. Sharpie in hand, I asked my husband what I should write on the outside of a new box. He said, *"I don't care, write whatever you want."*

This annoyed me, so I wrote "Happy Birthday Vince Lombardi." Some future grandchild will come across the holiday decorations and wonder, *"What in the world was wrong with my grandparents?"*

We cherish those ornaments given by friends and family. A college friend gave us an Indiana Gas Company bulb "Light up the holidays with gas." Santa Gator, from our Florida days, is a favorite, as well a beautiful red and gold ornament from the Hotel de Coronado in San Diego. We still have the Shell station Santa Claus from the best man in our wedding. He got it *free with a fill-up.*

When we had our only child, friends and family were so thrilled they gave us about half a dozen "Baby's First Christmas 1990" ornaments.

That baby is a man now, and yet we still display all the ornaments, including a tiny, construction paper, red hand, made by our son at Chandler Elementary School in kindergarten.

During our first Christmas season together as a married couple, my husband and I baked traditional holiday cookies. We also made a pitcher of homemade sangria in our one-bedroom Florida apartment that overlooked the neighborhood gun shop.

We made a second pitcher of sangria.

After the routine mixing, spooning and dropping of the batter, baking, cooling, and icing the cookies, we were up for anything. We put flour in our hair to see what the future held.

That amusement didn't last long. *Hmmm, what should we do next?*

We made a third pitcher of sangria.

We spied Bub, our first gray cat. Naturally, we floured the cat. What would he look like when he was older? The sangria had clouded our judgment.

At no time was Bub in danger. We gently kneaded some flour into his fur to see what he would look like with some age on him. Bub was not thrilled with his sudden aging and hid under the couch.

Now we are just days away from the special holidays. We no longer need to flour our hair; nature has taken care of that.

The tree is up with its diverse and special ornaments.

Happy Birthday, Vince Lombardi, and to all a good night.

CHAPTER TWENTY

Attack of the Day People

In my new work-at-home-life, I've discovered a sub-culture that exists outside of a full-time gig.

These are not Jane-Austen-loving-zombies or vampires who want to make sweet love and then bite your neck. Or are they?

This miraculous, undiscovered sub-culture is what I refer to as the Day People. I spent the last thirty years running from place to place during the work-day. Somehow I was oblivious to the archetypes I've seen repeated in my community during my few weeks away from the official work force.

Old Folks Drinking Coffee. In the formal work days, I zipped through one of the local coffee places at high speed. I chose among the usual suspects, Four-Bucks, local donut shop, or Mickey Dee's, depending on the numbers of cars in line.

The drive-up crew knew me by my car, recently my sparkle-blue Crest-toothpaste-colored fleet sedan, covered with the four-foot luminescent logos of my former employer.

Now, I have the time to go inside the coffee shop. They are inside, this whole sub-culture of people.

Here's the scary part: some of them are reading a daily newspaper. I did not say iPad; I said newspaper. I feel as if I've opened the door of the tombs in the Valley of the Kings.

Have you ever heard of anything so extreme?

It gets worse. Some of them are actually talking to each other.

They don't text or read anything on their cell phones. Some don't even have cell phones.

I've overheard them talking in their secret, cult language. They speak of Part B, dollar cost averaging, and predictably in a doughnut shop, doughnut holes. They also seem to be obsessed with the weather.

"Gonna rain, Bert?"

"Cold enough for you?"

"How about that frost last night?"

They talk a lot about sports, a mind-numbing discussion that sends me into a hypnotic state if I happen to overhear it. Occasionally, one of them will get up and head for a medical appointment. Friends watch Ernie drive away in his old Park Avenue Buick or Chevy Malibu, the one with the bumper sticker that says, "I love my grandbabies."

Don't get too cozy here because these people have eaten my brains.

The reason I know about them is that in just a few weeks I've become one of them. My unemployed or self-employed or retired friends invite me to join them at one of these places—on the <u>inside</u>. With the economic changes, more of my friends are unemployed or working from home and are also in this brave new post-corporate world.

My friends want to talk. To me. Not text or e-mail, but talk and have coffee. Have you ever heard of anything so radical? We rarely talk over "no whip, two pump, skinny mochas" anymore. In this new life, we order regular coffee, often with a coupon.

The ex-beauty queens. I frequently use a franchise mailing store. Today I was mailing holiday packages at mid-day and I waited behind two women, slightly younger than me. Before I entered the store, I had pulled up beside one of them in the parking lot. She drove a white Lexus SUV with one of those stickers of stick people on the rear window—two adults, two kids, and a dog.

I saw that she envied my car—a faded, red, eleven-year old Honda sedan with a left crushed fender *("Son, don't hit the side of the garage when you back out!")*

The two women in line knew each other, and I could not help but overhear their conversation.

"I'm sending Johnny a care package up at State University," said the first one, resplendent in a red snowman holiday vest, sporting perfect matching red nails, and white boots with fur around the tops.

"He was just home last weekend, but I know he and his buddies will enjoy all these Christmas decorations during finals week."

She piled about a dozen Toblerone bars, a two-foot decorated Christmas tree, Sun Chips, and a box of tinsel on the counter.

"I'm so silly, I know he is coming home in a few days, but I just miss him soooo much."

The second woman asked, *"When will he get his grades?"*

"In about ten days," said Miss Kokomo 1987, *"He refused to give up his own password so I did it for him. Can you believe it? Now he has to type 'I love my Mom Janet' every time he checks his e-mail. Isn't that adorable?"*

"Adorable," echoed the other woman.

My skull cracked open, cerebral tissue seeping, oozing out.

73

It is happening; my brains are literally being sucked from my head cavity by The Day People. My brains run down my body, over my American University blue T-shirt down to my Walgreens sale sweatpants and onto my plaid, high-top Tasmanian Devil Keds shoes.

Her friend, who had that perfect shade of blonde hair, the shade I paid eighty dollars a month for when I had the lucrative Fortune 100 job, said, *"By the way, is he still dating Chelsea? I saw her mother at the club last weekend and she didn't say one word to me."*

The first woman laughed as she flipped back her hair in the perfect Cover Girl toss.

She made it to the head of the line, and the clerk handed her the UPS form.

"Oh, my God, I don't even know Johnny's address," she said. *"Mind if I use your computer?"*

Three more people stepped in line behind me, behind the two perfect zombies.

I knew these women. I remembered. They were the same two ex-cheerleaders who insisted that the PTA meet in the daytime instead of evening. I met them at kindergarten roundup at my son's school in 1995. I served on a hospital management team and worked long hours.

I left without completing my business. They were eating my brains, I swear. Beware; be warned about The Day People. They will eat your brains and then spit you out in a perfect Waterford crystal vase.

CHAPTER TWENTY-ONE

Wheel of Misfortune

Every night, my husband and I watch *Wheel of Fortune*. We've watched it every night for the past twenty-mumble-mumble years.

I prefer *Jeopardy* but it is on during the day, and I swear when we do play it on a rare vacation day, my reference librarian spouse gets the plum categories. Today's categories were *NBA*, *Libraries*, *White People from Indiana*, *Mustache Grooming*, and *All Mahler All the Time*. I didn't have a chance, especially with Final Jeopardy.

Answer:

"Schotzie, big ugly dog belonging to Cincinnati Reds owner Marge Schott."

"Dang, a baseball question. I'll never get it."

And the question was:

"Who pooped on home plate prior to the 1990 World Series?"

But, tonight and every night we watch *Wheel of Fortune*. The high definition colors sweep across the TV screen and wiseacre Pat Sajak steps out with Vanna White.

Vanna always wears a Bob Mackie-esque dress (think Carol Burnett on her old show) and enters in a flourish to the excited applause of the studio audience.

During the introductions, my impatient husband wants to answer some questions so he flips the channel to *Who Wants to Be a Millionaire* and then grouses about the format change.

He turns back to *Wheel*.

The category is "Philadelphia" and tonight's first puzzle is XXXXXXXXXXX XX XXXXXXXXXXXX.

Before anyone guesses it, my spouse yells out "Declaration of Independence." I'm still trying to read the category, "Name."

His quick answer ticks me off, and I steam a little bit inside, thinking of some manipulative ways for revenge. *Maybe I'll put a Plastic # 2 bottle in the Glass recycling bin! That'll teach him!*

After the first round and commercials for constipation products, Depends, erectile dysfunction, and incontinence drugs, Pat introduces the contestants.

I hate this part.

Hello, Pat, my name is Sadie Sadie Married Lady, and I'm married to my wonderful husband Irving for 13 years and we're here with our awesome children, Whitney, Sidney, and Kelsey. My hobby is rescuing baby kittens and I work for a large unnamed company that processes dairy products.

And Pat says "Awesome" and Vanna nods with delight.

Now just how freaking cheesy is that?

How about a regular contender who is a real person?

Hello, Pat, my name is Betty and I've been divorced from my alcoholic, worthless, lazy husband Norbert for ten years and that sonnovabitch left me with these two worthless children, Norbert Junior and Nora Beth. Neither of them could be here today because they are doing community service for pot possession. I've been unemployed for six years, long before being unemployed was accepted, and I'm about to lose my under-water house to the bank.

And Pat says, "Awesome" and Vanna nods with delight.

My husband solves more puzzles. The category is now "Before and After" and the display reads XXXXXX XXXXXXX XXXX.

Before I can comprehend the spaces for three words, he shouts out *"Robert Lincoln Logs!"*

That is correct, but the television contestants take four more minutes, and Sadie Sadie the Married Lady, wins the Prize Puzzle. She is thrilled to learn that she will explore Kentucky, Indiana, and Illinois to see Robert Lincoln's entire ancestral homeland.

"This prize package, which includes a week at the Dale, Indiana Super 8, is worth eight thousand, four hundred, and sixty-two dollars," says Pat and the contestant jumps in joy.

The winner is ultimately chosen and taken to the small wheel. Pat introduces her lovely and awesome family.

"Who do you have with you tonight?" The camera switches to the audience, where Sadie's family stands proudly but uncomfortably, and looking like rubes, so in awe of the glory of Pat and Vanna.

My family could do this well. We have proudly looked like rubes for generations.

This is the part of the show that I find really objectionable. No matter the gender of the contestant, Pat guides him or her from the small wheel to the big board. For a female, he takes her hand. I've watched this show hundreds, if not thousands, of times. What female cannot figure out how to go from the small wheel to the big board?

It's not as if the place isn't well lighted.

Sometimes I fantasize about what I would do if Pat Sajak took my hand, leading me to the big board. My husband believes that my admission that I fantasize about <u>this</u> is enough evidence to lock me up for a mighty long time. I think I would just smack Pat away, but who knows?

The final thing that makes me crazy is the idiotic banter between Pat and Vanna at the very end of the show. The producers are most likely shouting, *"Kill some time."*

Vanna usually shows a picture of her children at Vail or St. Thomas, while Pat makes an incredibly snarky comment. You know he is thinking of the 1970s Steve Martin comedy routine, *"I get paid for doing this."*

CHAPTER TWENTY-TWO

My Weekly Readers

In Miss Enid Heckman's third-grade class, we received a weekly newspaper written for elementary schoolchildren. In 1965, "My Weekly Reader" was to this word-hungry eight-year-old what *The New Yorker* is today to this word-hungry fifty-something.

I subscribe to several weeklies and read all I can find. Community journalism still, I believe, has an important place in a fast-paced world of social media.

Today's lead story in the weekly where I live is "Call before You Dig." Last week, someone in a trailer park hit a gas line when digging.

In a weekly, don't miss the weddings or the obits, which generally provide much greater detail than the dailies. The advertisements themselves are interesting, all locally produced, and often featuring family members. "Jim and Bev, owners of the John Deere Lawn Mower Store, welcome their new grandson Billy to the lawn mower business."

The New Yorker's Talk of the Town should be so detailed.

This week's cover photo in the paper where I grew up features a picture of a fifth grader pulled on a skateboard by his dog, enjoying the last playtimes of a summer day.

I grew up in a rural area, which had two dailies and three weeklies. Fifty years ago, we counted on newspapers for much of our news, backed up by radio and television. Circulation was much larger for most newspapers than it is today and many newspapers have folded.

The two dailies where I grew up merged and I'm uncertain how many of the weeklies remain.

I subscribe to my hometown weekly, where I once worked as a prepubescent Lois Lane.

When I was fourteen, my Dad finagled a job at a weekly for me. He knew the office manager, who knew everything and everybody in my small town.

Rosalie Stellar chased all over this town of 1,200 people with her heavy German camera and even heavier flash attachment to report on local events. She hired local high school kids every summer for minimum wage.

I rode my bike to cover school stories and wrote the "School News" column. My work was riveting—especially my awe-inspiring prose on the Library Club acquisition of a new display window.

The gracious Rosalie taught me to operate the string machine that bundled the papers every Wednesday morning. I learned to answer the phones and how to count words for classified advertising. I learned how to proofread legal ads set in five point type.

Two men owned the weekly. They tapped out Linotype on ancient, rickety machines in the back while Rosalie ran the front office. At noon, the "boys" closed up the back shop and went to the tavern next door for lunch.

I only lasted one summer at this newspaper, swayed by the money and glamour of carhopping at the local Dog and Suds.

While Rosalie and the "boys" are long gone, the newspaper content has not changed much in forty years.

Each week the paper prints the names of those persons who have newly subscribed or are renewing subscriptions. No one in my family lives there anymore, but we all still get the paper.

My favorite part is the "Memories of Long Ago" column. Last week my aunt was mentioned in the "Sixty-Five Years Ago" section. The article reported my aunt won first prize in a home economics demonstration contest at the county fair. My aunt moved away from Indiana in 1949.

Sometimes the old columns are fun—sometimes they are poignant. I anticipate the summer of 2011 as some of my stunning early work may hit the "Forty Years Ago" column.

More often, the columns remind me of the fragility of life. Several weeks ago I read in the "Forty Years Ago" column that a young man I knew then enlisted in the United States Marines.

He didn't come home from the war, but forty years ago we didn't know that yet. He was just an innocent, fresh-faced eighteen-year-old from a small town in Indiana, going off to a country we could barely find on the map: South Vietnam.

CHAPTER TWENTY-THREE

Chickens Coming Home to Roost

Sometimes when we drive to work together before eight a.m., my husband and I barely talk, or simply speak at each other in monosyllabic grunts. This quiet time reflects nothing on our long-term, happy relationship—it reflects that we are <u>not</u> morning people. At that hour, I've not had any coffee yet for I am too lazy to get up and make it and too worried about hard water build-up to make it the night before.

This week the drive has been dismal. As we opened the garage door both our glasses steamed up from the oppressive humidity. That level of intensive humidity before eight in the morning does not portend well for the coming week. The heat is exhausting and makes us both a little cranky. Correction, a lot cranky.

Monday we drove past some new neighbors, and a peacock strutted in their front yard. The stylish bird showed full frontal plumage, in all the essential peacock colors.

I looked at husband out of a half-opened eye and grunted, *"Was that what I thought it was?"*

"Hmmm," the man of a few morning words said, *"A peacock?"*

Nothing else was said, though I thought it was odd to see a peacock in the neighbor's yard.

Were we hallucinating because of the heat, like parched soldiers in a desert creating an oasis ahead? In this early morning heat, we could have seen The Rolling Stones performing in the neighbor's yard and responded with equally monosyllabic grunts.

Tuesday morning the blast furnace effect of summer hit us as we opened the garage door before work. Driving past the same neighbors, we saw ten or twelve laying hens of different colors on the front lawn.

This is something you don't often see in our neighborhood. Granted we are not a gated community; we have no fancy brick sign with a name carved on it like River Oak or Monosyllabic Manor. Most of the homes in our neighborhood are thirty years old, and they are aging. Originally, this neighborhood of custom homes catered to doctors and lawyers. Today, teachers and social workers and factory workers live in this Unnamed Suburban Neighborhood.

We still retain some of the grace of a once upscale neighborhood. Nearly all the mailboxes are mounted in brick and we all have concrete driveways. Yards are well maintained and overall well landscaped. There are no refrigerators on the front porch, junky trucks in the driveway, decorative trolls in the front yards, or even pole barns. Most of us own yard barns that look like real barns, red or brown with white trim.

Only one crazed homeowner has a tacky concrete dinosaur, hiding in a discreet rock garden at the back of the house.

But chickens?

Chickens lay eggs, I'm told. I learned from my dad, a high school agriculture teacher, that's where eggs come from. I grew up in farm country, and I've made the connection between chicken and egg (though never solved the 'which came first' conundrum.)

But chickens?

86

I missed something here. I thought the chickens might be missing something also, because I had not heard a rooster yet. Maybe the peacock knows something we don't know.

This agriculture teacher's daughter needed no explanation of why chickens are necessary for eggs.

Calling on a physician client at lunch yesterday, I mentioned the strangeness of chickens in our suburban neighborhood and the lack of a rooster.

The physician, a man who took college courses in science for at least a dozen years, asked me, *"What about the eggs?"*

I explained that Americans eat unfertilized eggs, and therefore no rooster is needed in the equation. In a suburban neighborhood, it is unnecessary for egg production, and mostly annoying for the neighbors.

Some Asian countries eat—and even pay more for—the treat of fertilized eggs.

In this country, we call those chicks.

Perhaps the next issue will be a neighborhood chopping block. For readers who have never witnessed a chicken extermination, here's my synopsis based on long-repressed memories from childhood.

There are five easy steps:

1. Neck on chopping block. (Thus the origination of the phrase, "running around like a chicken with her head cut off.")
2. Feet up, neck down on clothesline, draining blood.
3. Feathers plucked.
4. Chicken cleaned.

5. Fried, fricasseed, baked, broiled, grilled, pick your poison.

Voila! Sunday chicken dinner courtesy of one wicked grandmother and her trusty hatchet!

Tomorrow it is going to be 98 degrees with a heat index of 110. God only knows what we will see at the neighbor's house.

What next? Two of every species? I hope so; we could use the rain.

CHAPTER TWENTY-FOUR

My Dirty Little Secret is Diamond Shaped

Anyone who spends any time in the work world has had a job that wasn't exactly a dream job. We've all been there. I've been working for more than forty years, and I've had my share of awful jobs.

Every job has its own war stories—we think back upon our experiences and remember the highest highs and the lowest lows.

In a galaxy far, far away, I sold pharmaceuticals to physicians. After working in the health care industry for nearly twenty years, I fell into a sales job, almost by accident.

I went to a "cattle call" in Louisville, with hundreds of other applicants. As the day wore on, applicants moved forward or were dismissed. The process had shades of *Let's Make a Deal* or *The Lady and the Tiger*. I survived four rigorous interviews, and moved right on into a territory near my home. I was offered a salary with potential bonus nearly double what I was making, amazing benefits, a fleet vehicle, travel, and lovely parting gifts if I spun the wheel correctly.

I was hired because of my experience in women's health and women's hospitals. For the first few years, I exclusively promoted women's health products to obstetricians, gynecologists and family doctors who cared for a large female population. The job was awesome, and I loved it. I was able to travel all over the country, attend women's health conferences, and I was successful selling women's health products.

When I changed careers from health marketing to health sales, I only had one caveat. I did not want to sell an erectile dysfunction drug.

89

I talked to everyone and anyone about birth control, hormone replacement therapy, hot flashes, or female infertility. Yet, I had no desire to talk with physicians and other medical personnel about products that related to the male anatomy.

Now I'm a married woman, so I've been to the neighborhood. But not living there, I just didn't feel comfortable talking about the subject at length.

Waiting to meet another rep for breakfast one morning, I noticed the Denny's newspaper box. The headline read something like, *"Gigantic Global Pharma Company buys little Pharma Company."*

Employees of these companies—because of potential insider trading—are always the last to know. My little company was being gobbled up by one of the largest companies in the world.

Only two years after the "cattle call," I had to interview again for my own job because of the purchase of my company. After a long ten months of waiting to hear my fate, I learned I was now an employee of Gigantic Global Pharma, which did not have a women's health division.

Guess what division I was assigned? If you said, "men's health" you win a prize! And guess what my lead product was? If you said, "an erectile dysfunction drug," you win another prize!

Three issues are hard to contend with in selling an erectile dysfunction product—the jokes, the literature, and the giveaways.

Believe me, there is not a joke, poster, e-mail, sight-gag that I've not seen firsthand for this type of product.

How about the viral e-mail with the light switch? Light switch on or off, up or down. Seen it.

There's the one about the traveling salesman and the farmer's daughter and the little pill. Been there, sold that.

The literature is, shall we say, hard-core? For someone who found it challenging to say words representing the mail anatomy, this was interesting. Management dictated we use a chart delineating the four stages of an erection.

Approached as a serious medical condition, all is well. But, if you lose your cool, that is not good. Remarkably, I did well selling the drug. I am certain the secret to my success is that I was not the person some see as the typical pharmaceutical rep. There is not much similarity between me and the character "Julie" played by Heather Locklear on *Scrubs*. Most of my customers probably thought of me as their older sister.

During my tenure in Big Pharma, I attended a program where a witty urologist discussed the little-known fifth, or "diamond-cutter stage" of erection.

He was kidding. Thankfully, there was no chart or patient profile I had to present in offices, outlining the mythical stage five.

I often objected to the scatological humor male colleagues let loose at sales meetings. When I sold the erectile dysfunction drug, I was the lone female in a district of nine males.

Before the industry self-regulated with the PhARMA Code, erectile dysfunction drug giveaways were highly sought after. One infamous pen, not from my company, was made of a wood laminate and folded in half. Pulled apart, the pen opened slowly.

Among the popular items were scrub shirts, ties, computer mice that looked like race cars, and of course, the highly desired sticky notes.

Now I'm out of the business, having become one of the Great Unwashed when the Gigantic Global Pharma Company cut the sales force in half. Oh, but the stories I can tell. I am left with my stories and a bunch of very strange pens.

CHAPTER TWENTY-FIVE

No Snakes in the Mattress

We went shopping for a new mattress today and freaked out about the price. We were <u>not</u> spending four grand on a name-brand memory-foam mattress. I don't think I could ever sleep on it, knowing that it cost that much when we are paying for college tuition.

So, we bought a generic rip-off memory-foam mattress with matching memory-foam pillows. I was terrified it was made in a labor camp in outer Siberia and full of snakes *(get these muthaflipping snakes outta my muthaflipping mattress.)*

The salesman said it was made in Denver.

This would be the fourth bed of our married lives.

It was a king-sized bed, unlike the first double bed in which we spooned and cuddled. Now we both snore like freight trains and have at least one and often two cats between us.

The last mattress we bought was eighteen years ago. I still like it, but it was time for it to go. When selling prescription allergy medicine, I learned in training that mattresses weigh much more going out the door than coming in. Dust mites burrow into the mattress and over the years, dust mite corpses make the mattress heavier.

I've since told several people this charming tale. All have told me a version of *"Well, my mattress is completely covered with a giant Baggie, polyurethane, Saran Wrap."* Leave it to friends to make me sad and inadequate about the state of my outgoing mattress.

The bed before the one we're replacing was a water bed. The water bed is a challenge for anyone in the third trimester of pregnancy. Getting in and out of that bed, I resembled the White Star Line launch of the Titanic at Southampton.

Two months later

Thankfully, the new mattress did not contain any snakes. But from the moment it was in our bedroom, it had a life of its own.

The mattress stunk to high heaven—like a combination of teenage boy's feet, cigars, and mildew. The mattress came with a special kit for the purpose of deodorizing. Doesn't that seem odd, that a new mattress needs to be deodorized?

After buying this mattress, I went online and discovered that a memory-foam mattress is probably not the best choice for people with asthma and allergies.

Back at the mattress store, the salesman told us memory-foam mattresses often have a distinct odor when new.

No graduate of the Dale Carnegie School, the salesman made us feel stupid and condescended to us that *"everyone knows that these mattresses smell bad."*

Because they (the mattress, not the salesman) are petroleum based, memory-foam mattresses are subject to something called "off-gassing."

Now I am quite familiar with the concept of "off-gassing" as I have a husband, father, brother, son, and seven nephews.

This is apparently something different, but I didn't like it just the same.

The mattress salesman convinced us to give it more time and suggested we air out the room. This was difficult to do in January when we had five winter storms in a row, but we were patient.

We could not stand it any longer and we went back to the mattress store again. The mattress salesman wanted to send someone out to inspect the smell.

That's a new one for me: *"Hello, I'm the Mattress Inspector here to make sure you didn't cut off that little tag sewn on the mattress at the factory."*

We said *no and get that stinky thing out of our house.*

While we were there, we bought a new platform bed to go with the mattress. Most new mattresses are eighteen inches thick now. I felt like the maiden in *The Princess and the Pea*, ascending to my own bed each evening.

We found a platform bed and a new eighteen-inch mattress, a more traditional kind.

Finally, the new bed and new mattress arrived.

The delivery men ripped the protective plastic off the mattress; I buried my face into the plush pillow-top to sniff out any odor ogres.

No off-gassing. No bad smell. No apparent muthaflipping snakes in the muthaflipping mattress.

The delivery men set the mattress up on the new bed. We were surprised to see how high it came up. The new mattress on the new bed was about twelve inches higher than it seemed in the store.

The delivery man told me, *"Oh, the salesman should have told you to get the low-profile box springs."*

Gee, I could-a had a V-8!

Back to the drawing board.

Monday I will have to call the salesman back. Unless we want to continue making a running start before taking that giant leap into our bed each night, we're going to have to do something else. We want the low-profile box springs. I am getting way too old for these hi-jinks. (Only someone over fifty would use the word "hi-jinks.")

CHAPTER TWENTY-SIX

Old Bessie et al

I'm not into cars. If it gets me there, I'm okay with that. My first car was a 1971 Cutlass S my grandfather gave me. I called her "Old Bessie." Her most useful attribute was that she could hold about ten inebriated college friends who needed a Designated Driver or a trip to Dunkin' Donuts at three a.m.

My husband and I have owned numerous cars during our quarter-of-a-century marriage. Right after we were engaged, my betrothed bought a 1973 red Volkswagen Beetle. He traded in his beat-up Pontiac LeMans, tying up the muffler with a coat hanger on the way to the used car lot.

He took me for a test drive in the VW, on a wide, multi-lane boulevard in Clearwater, Florida. As soon as we pulled out of the used car lot, I asked him, *"Do you know how to drive a stick shift?"*

He said, *"Not really,"* and peeled out of the lot, squealing the tires.

My elderly grandmother also lived in Clearwater. One day after he left work he picked her up and brought her to my apartment. When they arrived, I asked her, *"Grammy, how did you like your ride over here in the Volkswagen?"*

Deadpan, she said, *"It was great, especially when we turned the corner on two wheels."*

My husband didn't have much luck with that car. In a two-month period, the VW was damaged while he was minding his own business driving to work on a Clearwater Street. In nearly identical accidents, two huge vehicles blew past him, heavy doors flying open and damaging the smaller, lighter Bug.

We paid $500 for the car, had several $500 collision repairs, fixed the transmission for $500, and sold the car for $500. After a few years, we had several grand invested in that little car.

Our "good" car was a 1981 Chevette. Our "good" car didn't have air conditioning, and we lived in Florida for more than two years without a.c. in our vehicles. After getting married, we traded in the Chevette. Being married now, and theoretically adults, we wanted a sedan and air conditioning.

For some reason that escapes me, we wanted a "K" car. Yes, the infamous "K" car, the one that comedians of the 1980s railed against, the most maligned vehicle of the era. The car was a ridiculous-looking metal box made of old Pepsi cans, aluminum foil balls, rubber bands, and Turkish taffy.

For the record, my husband now buys our cars, and I don't even go to the dealership with him. The reason is that I am gullible and easily influenced. I trust his judgment.

When we were newlyweds, I convinced my groom that the Dodge salesman, who told me he was from Indiana, was getting us the best deal.

We bought a new Dodge Aries, one of the legendary "K" cars (K stands for "Klunker" or "Krappy"). The car was a black, 4-door sedan. When you slammed the car door, the entire body shook.

Now living in Tampa, we took a shortcut home off Fletcher Avenue. Someone misplaced a huge box of roofing tacks because dozens of them punctured our new tires. All four of them. How special is it to get four flat tires on the way home from buying a new car?

A few weeks later I was driving home past a Temple Terrace golf course. Some duffer yards away hit a beautiful drive that sliced, smack into the right rear bumper of my car.

That car just seemed to ask for it.

CHAPTER TWENTY-SEVEN

The Church Directory Picture

Last Tuesday night we posed for our church directory picture.

The loquacious photographer told my husband repeatedly, *"What a lucky man you are!"*

We waited for the digital photo preview, and heard the photographer tell at least three more men the same thing. *"What a lucky man you are,"* he said again and again, whether their wives looked like Halle Berry or Broderick Crawford, same story.

The Sales Pitch man shooed us into the Sales Pitch room, normally a Sunday school room. The walls and tables were completely covered with framed pictures of happy, smiling families. Maybe there's something wrong with me, but I did not want to purchase dozens or even a single picture of us at this time in our lives.

We merely wanted to be in the church directory, to be recognized by other members in this growing church.

My husband may have gained a few pounds since college and his hair might be a bit thinner, but he still has the same sparkling blue eyes and radiant crooked smile. When I look at him I see George Clooney—love, after all, is blind.

As for me, I admit I have gained weight—is nineteen years long enough to lose the "baby weight?" I have several chinny chin chins. Two-inch hairs often grow from the middle of my cheek; and of course, one leaped forth right before the photo session last week.

I have stopped coloring my hair so I now have "salt and pepper" locks, unrecognizable from the bottle blonde I was. Now I use that purple rinse shampoo, the same one I made fun of when my mom and her friends used it.

When I needed new glasses, choosing the stylish Vera Bradley frames seemed a good idea. Now the frames are five years old, not at all stylish and look like they are from Kremlin Collection of 1963, with heavy-duty frames accented with my mannish eyebrows. In middle age, I look like a candidate for the Soviet leadership team.

Thanks to childhood summers at the lake, I have age spots in the shape of eastern European countries on my cheek. I have a 10x make-up mirror in my bathroom, surrounded by lights as bright as the klieg lights from an airport runway. I don't use make-up anymore; I use spackling paste from Lowe's with a hint of beige.

Did we want to buy a photographic representation of this?

No, we just wanted to be in the church directory.

Meanwhile, the Sales Pitch man continued his spiel—a 16 x 20 in a gold-leaf frame with the photo painted on a special canvas.

The Sales Pitch man said, *"Wouldn't this look great in your son's dorm room, don't you think?"*

Had this salesman lost his ever-loving mind? We're just happy that our college-age son acknowledges our existence; we don't think he really wants a larger-than-life-size photo of us in his college room.

We told the Sales Pitch man we were only interested in the free 8 x 10. We were just trying to make him happy; we weren't even really interested in that. Who would want it? I knew it would sit in our church mailbox for years until some future maintenance man threw it away.

We just wanted to be in the church directory. That is all.

The desperate Sales Pitch man now pleaded, *"Well, that photo is absolutely free. There is no additional cost; however, if you want the touch-up, it's only $29.95."*

Was he implying that we needed the touch-up?

He showed us two sample pictures. Each was of the same woman, but the untouched photograph highlighted wrinkles, age spots, discolorations, eye bags. The woman looked as wretched as a Disney cartoon witch.

In the retouched photograph, she was beautiful, even glowing. All for $29.95.

Both of us had the feeling that the Sales Pitch man really wanted us to do the retouching. Would his offer, as my husband said, include the little known *"mercy clause"* and give us the retouching for free?

He did not give us the free retouching, so we walked.

Out in cyberspace somewhere, perhaps as a bad example for some other church directory, is a reasonable likeness of George Clooney and the beloved Soviet leader.

CHAPTER TWENTY-EIGHT

Great Moments in Art

Today my sweetie and I spent a vacation day at the National Gallery in Washington, DC. Being inside the cool marble building is a great way to escape the dog days of summer. To paraphrase Dr. Seuss, "Oh, the places we did go!" We saw wonderful masterpieces by European and American artists, including some very famous pieces. How art fills the soul!

But, the day wasn't without its difficulties.

We are the two stupidest people on the face of the earth. Mostly me.

We decided to take the "Director's Tour" and rented two electronic devices that are tape players with recorded comments about the art. By typing in a three-digit number on an infinitesimally small screen, you can learn the curator's thoughts on the painting and artist, as well as historical context. The recorders, worn around the neck on a lanyard, are simple to operate, assured the nice man who rented two to us.

He reassured us when we looked confused, "*Any eight-year-old can do this.*"

After several hours, we broke for lunch and put the devices on our lunch table. After lunch we returned to the far galleries where our self-guided tour had stopped.

I tried to clear my machine by pressing the black square button, just like I did all morning. The machine is equipped with comments in four languages, English, French, Spanish, and Chinese.

Something went wrong, and I accidentally changed mine to French.

I don't understand French.

Foreign languages are not my forte. I lasted just one year in Mr. Kidd's high school Spanish I class, and kept getting in serious trouble with my childhood friend Michael, also a teacher's kid. When Mr. Kidd turned his back, Michael or I would adjust the dials on his audio master board. Volume on the teacher's headset rose way up or dropped way down to a whisper.

This made Mr. Kidd pretty mad.

What can I say? I was fourteen and a teacher's child. My friend Michael was also a teacher's child. Teacher's children often exhibit squirrely behavior with other teachers whom they have known since being in diapers.

Michael also liked to haphazardly flip the pages of our sophomore English teacher's book—Mrs. Lenwell might be lecturing from a text of "Macbeth." When the teacher turned her back, Michael turned the page and we moved right from the ugly witches and their brew to the agony of Lady Macbeth's hand washing. Do you notice a theme here?

In the art museum today, my husband got impatient with me and grabbed my machine.

He said, *"Let me take that one, I can fix it."*

So we traded. Within ten seconds of trading with my husband, I had changed his machine to French also. I'm trouble; I just can't help myself.

My husband doesn't speak French either, though he did say a few choice words to me that may have been in a foreign tongue. He was unable to *"fix"* either of them so I returned to the helpful person who told us the machines were *"simple and easy."*

The clerk took the two machines from me and couldn't fix them. He said, *"What did you do to these?"* and gave me two new ones.

He then said, *"Au revoir."* That's French for, *"Get the heck out of my face."*

CHAPTER TWENTY-NINE

Home Cooking

This afternoon we saw *Julie and Julia*. New Yorker Julie Powell works her way through *Mastering the Art of French Cooking* in one year, blogs about her adventures, and discovers her writing chops. She is rewarded with a book contract and a major motion picture starring Oscar-winning actress Meryl Streep.

Why hasn't this happened to me? I've been cooking my way through a stack of cookbooks for more than four decades.

Take the St. John's Lutheran Cookbook, for example. My grandmother's recipe for Christmas rum balls is featured in the dessert section. The recipe calls for two teaspoons of rum flavoring.

Flavoring? I don't think so.

Eating one of those stout little gems was a nice pick-me-up before Christmas Eve service and is probably what encouraged an amorous Martin Luther to jump over the nunnery fence and retrieve Sister Katharina, his future wife.

When I was a child, the church was known for homemade ice cream socials and fish fry's. The Men's Club recipe for potato salad is also included in this cookbook. I'm reprinting it here in case you are hosting hundreds of people for lunch tomorrow.

Potato Salad:

250 lbs. of potatoes

35 dozen eggs, boiled

10 stalks of celery

10 quarts of sweet pickles

10 large sweet onions

Dressing:

3 quarts of mustard

2 1/2 quarts of vinegar

10 cans of Milnot

5 lbs of sugar

4 1/2 gallons of Miracle Whip

(Important editor's note: do not substitute mayonnaise for Miracle Whip if you intend to hold true to your Hoosier heritage. Hoosiers don't use mayonnaise—it is against an unwritten moral code.)

Boil, peel, and chop potatoes. Add chopped eggs, celery, pickles, and onions. Mix well. Mix all ingredients for salad dressing and put in large containers.

Another recipe in the cookbook calls for "one mango, chopped fine." I know that "mango" means green pepper in Indiana, and in the rest of the world it means a fruit. Some of the other recipes from this cookbook are white sausage brain pudding, northern plain tomato rabbit, and a cake with a cup of hickory nuts.

Where do you get hickory nuts? If your answer is Euell Gibbons, you are dating yourself, and it just isn't funny.

The cookbook also contains a recipe for mincemeat, a distinctly German Lutheran hamburger, raisins, and a sugary substance used to make pies. My grandmother and mother participated in mincemeat parties, focusing on socializing and pie-making.

Thumbing through this cookbook is like talking with three generations of women—my grandmother, my mother, and I belonged to the church at different times between 1936 and 2002. Between the three of us, we knew most of the women represented in the cookbook, which was published in the 1970s.

Many women featured in the cookbook have now earned their eternal reward, making lebkuchen and canned mincemeat with their sisters in the big German kitchen upstairs. Reviewing these recipes is like visiting old friends whom I can still imagine laughing while washing and putting away dishes in the tiny church kitchen.

CHAPTER THIRTY

When in Rome

While visiting Hot Springs, Arkansas last weekend, I bought a spa package to experience the local flavor. Hot Springs is famous for its "Bathhouse Row" where gangsters and society doyennes alike "took the waters." I took my parents to Arkansas for a short vacation; it is difficult for my dad to travel with my mother who has dementia. She requires bathroom support on a trip, and it is nice for Dad to have an extra driver.

For most of the six-day trip, the three of us were together.

Downtown Hot Springs is a national park. We visited a restored bathhouse from an earlier era and saw a colorful stained-glass ceiling, which featured mermaids and Neptune's Daughter.

For centuries, the curative powers of the waters of Hot Springs drew the ailing and the curious. In the early 1900s, the magic powers may have resulted from the prescribed fourteen days of bathing. In most of America then, a Saturday evening bath in the family's washtub behind the kitchen stove was the norm. In Hot Springs, two weeks of bathing, plus the required strolling on the Boardwalk brought healing to many with arthritis and other pains.

Before our long drive home, I had a mineral bath, massage, and scrub at our hotel spa. A large, tiled room featured a pristine, marbled jet tub. The attendant showed me various bath oils and I chose juniper.

Immediately the sparkling waters filled the tub with bubbles. Getting into this tub was so totally decadent, like a fantasy of how the perfect bubble bath should be. The tub was surrounded with small, lighted candles, and mellow music set the scene.

As I sat down Buddha-like in the effervescent water, my bulk caused the bubbles to rise almost over my head. An imaginary visitor could only see my seemingly disembodied head, floating in the bubbles.

I had a massage, exfoliating scrub, and then the most refreshing shower of my life. The water is purportedly 130 degrees and has to be cooled for showers.

Nearly eight p.m., the attendant suggested I return to my room in my bathrobe.

"What a great idea," I thought, *"Then, I can put my pajamas on, and continue this amazing feeling of relaxing in the room."*

I gathered my clothes in a terry cloth bag provided by the spa, and wrapped up in the fluffy, white robe, and hobbled in my spa slippers to the elevator. The electronic doors opened and I went into the empty elevator. As the doors shut behind me, I remembered *"I am staying at an Embassy Suites!"*

Ever stayed at an Embassy Suites with their huge, open atrium, and glass elevators?

Had I unclenched my terrycloth bag to press the elevator's "open" button, I am sure my too-tight robe would have flapped in the breeze. Since it was around eight p.m., most of the men attending a plumbing convention were wrapped around the piano bar in the atrium.

Beep. I backed up slowly and clutched my clothing bag against my chest to hold the robe shut, and I closed my eyes until we reached the eighth floor.

CHAPTER THIRTY-ONE

No Enchanted Evening

The beach was waiting for us, though not the craggy, pocked coast of Hawaii featured in *From Here to Eternity.*

Clearwater Beach on this chilly New Year's Eve offered white sands as slick as Splenda and the beckoning, mysterious waters of the Gulf of Mexico beyond.

I dreamed of this evening months in advance, conjuring up images of great movie romances, including the beach-soaked scene with Deborah Kerr and Burt Lancaster in *From Here to Eternity.*

New Year's Eve 1982 was going to be our romantic introduction to a great new year, and we would celebrate locking lips on north Clearwater Beach.

Always fantasizing that I'm a heroine in a movie, I waited for my White Knight to come along just like Marian Paroo's Harold Hill in *The Music Man.* Except in my scenario, the White Knight is the librarian (my reference librarian husband as Darian the Librarian) and I'm the slick sales person.

There I am on the footbridge with Robert Preston breathing down my neck.

In *The Sound of Music*, Eleanor Parker stands on that Austrian mansion balcony and says to Christopher Plummer, *"Somewhere out there is a young woman who I think….is never going to be a nun."*

Then I'm Sister Maria, vulnerable and trembling in the garden gazebo with Captain von Trapp. They sing "Something Good." I really don't believe Maria had a "wicked childhood."

Or I'm Mitzi Gaynor as Ensign Nellie Forbush having "Washed That Man Right Outta My Hair." Yet, the girl who is as corny as Kansas in springtime overcomes her prejudices, falling madly in love with Rossano Brazzi's Emile de Becque in *South Pacific*.

I am Deborah Kerr, whether kissing Burt Lancaster on that island beach or dancing with Yul Brenner in *The King and I*. When the waves crashed upon them, it was like the crescendo in a Wagnerian opera, all the muses in perfect form, sight, touch, sound frantically rushing in the waves.

Oh, how my mind plays tricks on me, because in my little 1982 drama I'm more like some intrepid combination of Marjorie Main, Kathy Bates, and Alice the Goon. As much as I want us to be Fred Astaire and Ginger Rogers, we are Fred and Wilma Flintstone in orthotic shoes. Or worse, we are Ma and Pa Kettle from the old movies.

Even nerds need love.

Darian the Librarian moved to Florida to be with me, his new love. I flew to Indiana to visit my parents. Darian and I drove back to the Sunshine State together, in our own State of Bliss. It really wasn't a State of Bliss, but a broken-down 1973 Pontiac LeMans with the car bottom occasionally scraping the road.

Before we left, the two families met. Darian was not yet a librarian, but an unemployed journalist with a framed degree and a double major in English Literature and journalism.

My parents went with us to his brother's home where Darian's mother lived. Each family eyed the other with suspicion. My parents were not particularly delighted that this unemployed young man was moving to Florida for the alleged, worrisome State of Bliss.

After much awkward small talk about football, Florida oranges, and relatives, Darian's brother said, *"Oh, we have some relatives in Florida who are fruit pickers."*

My father looked at my mother and said, *"Marilyn, it's time to get on the road."*

Then they both got up and left me with the relatives of the seasonal workers.

Mind you, there is fruit that needs to be picked, and all work is good. Darian's brother was making small talk. These distant cousins hadn't darkened the door in thirty years.

Darian and I shoved his possessions in the trunk and left for the South. Not wanting to upset our parents, we didn't stop at a hotel. In retrospect, this seems ridiculous because after a 22-hour ride in an old car with poor shocks, romance was <u>not</u> the first thing on our minds.

We kept going, crossed the Courtney Campbell Causeway just after dawn. The waters of Tampa Bay gleamed against the Howard Frankland Bridge to the west (known as the Frankenstein to locals). We arrived at our new life—beyond the causeway was light and magic and hope and new love. From the darkness of that nearly sunrise-to-sunrise journey, we drove into the gleaming winter color of Pinellas County. Green palm trees, a blue sky, pink striped geraniums, orange marigolds, yellow nasturtium, white ornamental peppers, royal blue snapdragons, and red wax begonias, a view like Dorothy saw when opening the door from sepia to Technicolor in *The Wizard of Oz*.

I was Dorothy with my love in his 1973 Pontiac LeMans. What awaited us was our great unknown future, and all the optimism that young and foolish people embrace.

That night we packed for our beach date—a picnic basket with cheese, crackers, a bottle of champagne and a blanket. We needed no music as the gentle, lapping waves of the Gulf provided a romantic background overture to our lovely symphony.

Right at sunset we arrived on north Clearwater Beach.

We noticed people leaving the parking lot. The beach was deserted. Why, on this most glorious of nights?

We spread the blanket near the water, but the corners kept blowing up. Florida had a cold month, and the winds picked up as the darkness enveloped the sea and the sand.

We placed the picnic basket on one corner of the blanket, and planted ourselves to hold the blanket down. With darkness came frigid cold. Locals walked the beach, bundled up in heavy coats with hoodies up and scarves and gloves in place.

The gentle music of the waves we expected was more like a nor'easter blowing into Cape Cod.

The water was about the temperature the victims experienced in *Titantic*.

That was our rude introduction to the Real Florida, where no self-respecting native goes to the beach when it is forty-five degrees. Ma and Pa Kettle returned to the little Largo apartment next to the gun shop and played Monopoly with Ma's roommate.

May your New Year bring all the romance and magic you desire, just as you imagine.

CHAPTER THIRTY-TWO

Vows for Old Married People

There's a magical quality to the marriage ceremony of young people. The white dress, the sacred music, the brides of another era dabbing eyes with linen handkerchiefs only used for such an occasion, all contribute to the ambiance of the day.

In front of each other, the couple recite vows while friends and relatives watch, tearfully or tragically.

Break the glass, light the candle, jump the broom, or drink the wine.

Then, the real work begins.

The idea of getting remarried, or at least updating vows, may be of value for the long-term married couple.

Like the old sedan in the garage, old married couples may need a tune-up and possibly a new fan belt, but somehow keep chugging along. My husband and I have been married nearly twenty-eight years, and we still have a lot in us just like our twelve-year-old Honda. The paint is chipped and the fender bent, but the engine runs fairly well.

We've been faithful, obeyed each other in sickness and health—yada yada yada as Elaine says on *Seinfeld*.

So why not say vows for the second act? We need vows for a new time in our lives. I wouldn't mind going to Las Vegas and reciting them in front of an Elvis impersonator, but that's just me.

For Him:

I, State Your Name, continue to take thee to be my wedded wife, despite reservations that defy common sense.

121

To have and to hold from this day forward, or until the Mayan calendar ends,

For better, for when you mate my socks, or make refried beans for dinner,

For worse, when your relatives visit for days on end and want to control the TV remote,

For richer, for poorer, until Social Security and Medicare kick in, in sickness with your constant hot flashes or in health on those days when your hormones aren't raging and you actually behave somewhat normally,

To love you even when you constantly ask me inane questions about football or when you mess up my special remote on the big TV in the basement or forget to write down in the checkbook how much you spent for groceries,

To cherish you until death do us part and you cremate me and take my insurance money and go to Hawaii for a month with a younger man.

Thereto I plight thee my troth for at least another thirty years.

For Her:

I, State Your Name, continue to take thee as my wedded husband, even though I really don't like Sports Center or you running the channels constantly with the special $89 LED remote I can't understand,

To have and to hold from this day forward or until global warming sucks all the air and water from our universe,

For better, on those nights when we can read side by side while listening to Riverwalk Jazz,

Or worse, when we have to drive somewhere we are obligated to go, but it is dark and neither of us can see well,

For richer, when we were able to travel to Europe and pretend like we are of Royal Blood even if we are on a tour bus with thirty other Baby Boomers,

For poorer, when we sit at the kitchen table and try to figure out how to pay all the bills because I lost a good job three years ago and the business I started has its ups and downs,

In sickness, when you are crabby because you have a minor cold, and in health, when you are so happy you'll take all the recycling stuff to the dump by yourself on Saturday morning,

Thereto I plight thee my troth for another three decades or so of bad puns and silliness and staying up too late to watch Storage Wars *or* House Hunters.

For Him:

I will dig in my dresser drawer for that simple gold band we bought at Service Merchandise for around fifty dollars, and I'll look at it once in a while and remember that I am married.

For Her:

I'll wear my wedding ring, also purchased at Service Merchandise for around thirty dollars, to business functions where I want people to know I'm still married.

Voice of deceased minister who married this couple, though he's been in the St. Peter's Lutheran Cemetery for fifteen years:

By the power vested in me by the State of Indiana and the Lutheran Church, you are now good to go.

I now pronounce you Old Married People.

CHAPTER THIRTY-THREE

What I Learned from the Woods

I went to the woods because I wished to live deliberately, to front only the essential facts of life, and see if I could not learn what it had to teach, and not, when I came to die, discover that I had not lived.

Henry David Thoreau

We did not go to the woods for such esoteric reasons. We went to the woods sixteen years ago because we needed more space, and the house we bought was adjacent to a woods.

Over time I came to realize that this was not our property; we were merely interlopers. Our place is populated with a variety of critters, some seen and some unseen. But we know they are here. And they know we are here.

Take the groundhogs (please). We have yet to catch the most recent visitor that we frequently see sunning in the afternoons on the side lawn. We found the entrance to his lair and closed it off; it remains closed. That probably means he has just found another route into his secret hideaway.

One evening I opened the back door to our deck, heard a squeal, and saw a fur ball run directly past me. It was Mr. Groundhog, who did not like my closeness. The odd sound he made may explain why they are called groundhogs, because they squeal like pigs.

We have a trap used for the various beasts, but friends humanely relocate the captured to an Animal Witness Protection program. These friends cannot divulge the exact spot to us, or they would have to kill us.

Last summer the trap caught something, and it was the oddest-looking thing I've ever seen. Whatever it was had gray coloring with a pointy nose. We've spotted red foxes in our yard, but this was gray. I sent a picture to our county extension agent, speculating that it was a rare gray fox. Months later, when I went to the office to use the extension agent as a source for a news story, they were still laughing about the woman who was unable to recognize a young raccoon, or the "highly unusual gray-striped fox" as the agent called it.

Neither Mr. Raccoon nor his kin are welcome. Two years in a row we had raccoons get into our attic—the second year the coon made sport with our thirty-five-year old roof and we had to replace it.

Most of the United States is still overpopulated with white-tailed deer and our neighborhood is no exception. Until we built a fence across the back of our property, anywhere from four to seven deer crossed our yard after sunset each night. Our fence has only rerouted the inevitable, a neighbor commented that deer have now found his garden and are having their evening appetizers on their travels through his yard.

When we still had an outdoor cat, I opened the back door one evening to fill his bowl. Eating the remains of Tiger's breakfast was a nice fat opossum, three feet from my screened door. We had wondered why Tiger's bowl frequently needed a refill.

We've hosted the occasional large turtle. At our first home, my husband was mowing the lawn and nearly clipped a snapping turtle with a shell about a foot in diameter.

Our neighbors contribute to this zoo, with various dogs of all sizes and temperaments. The common breed is

126

domestic Crotch Rocket, as they all greet us in the same manner.

Four or five houses up the street we have an "urban chicken rancher" who has the world's horniest rooster and six or seven chickens that like to inhabit the middle of the road.

My husband, who thinks he is very funny, often pauses in the car and yells at them, *"Why, why?"* (as in *"Why does the chicken cross the road?"*)

These same neighbors also have peacocks which give the noisy rooster a run for his money. The peacocks fly from roof to roof, which often surprises visitors.

In calm weather, I enjoy sitting on the deck, though I've considered emulating Granny from *The Beverly Hillbillies* and protecting my turf from critters with a shotgun across my lap.

"Ya'll come back now, ya hear."

CHAPTER THIRTY-FOUR

Only the Good Dye Young

As we age, parts of us change color. We want our teeth white, but not our hair. We want our arms and legs bronze, but no brown age spots on our faces. We women deal with our shifting palette every day.

A few weeks ago I visited my father, who lives in a retirement home. Another resident saw me in the hall and asked me, *"Are you a new resident?"*

No, I am not a new resident, and I snarled at her in my head. Technically, I am old enough to live there, and I am aware that there are several residents my age.

There it is. I am eligible for AARP and have the right to buy the senior portions at Bob Evans. If I forget and shop on a Tuesday, the grocery store clerks asked me if I am eligible for the senior discount.

There's no disguising this fact of life. About four years ago I gave up coloring my hair to see what God hath wrought.

I can't afford $80 every four weeks for the joy of being a blonde. I had my own sorry history with drug-store dye products and wasn't successful with getting consistent color. So I let it go and within eight weeks, my hair was thoroughly gray.

Genes are, frankly, not my friend except in the area of skin and hair. My maternal grandmother and mother both aged with beautiful skin and silver-to-white hair, and it appears I'm on that track.

With her beautiful white hair tied in a French knot, my grandmother was mistaken for Maria von Trapp in Stowe,

Vermont. She loved the attention and did not correct the mistake. Had she been asked to sing, she most likely would have burst into song (revealing the deception).

My mane began to lighten when I was in my late twenties. I colored my own hair for many years, except for the nine months I was expecting. (Hide those hospital-with-baby photos.)

Coloring your own hair is a challenge. Women who say it's easy are lying or have a sister-in-law who is a stylist. Mark my words.

And while the hair gets whiter, the teeth go in the other direction. I've never been blessed with sparkling white teeth. My choppers were already yellowing when the orthodontist pulled off my braces in 1968.

I am a coffee drinker, and I know this compounds the issue. Without the daily pleasures of white sugar, flour, and real Coca-Cola, don't try to take my coffee away from me.

So what to do? On a friend's suggestion I recently tried activated charcoal capsules, a homeopathic fix.

My friend empties capsules of activated charcoal to make a paste or "slurry" to whiten her teeth. This may be an old wives tale, but I'm an old wife. Apparently the charcoal is quite corrosive and removes plaque. I've never tried to open a capsule before. There must be a trick to it, but I didn't know it, so I cut it open with cuticle scissors.

Surprise! Immediately after opening the capsule, black stuff flew everywhere on my white countertop. "Activated charcoal" is code for *black tar that sticks to everything.*

I opened another pill for enough to make a paste. Leaning over the sink, I put my brush into the oily ebony stuff and rubbed it against my ivories.

Having worn braces—both upper and lower bands and a face bow—for five years, I brush well. Apparently, I brush too well, and with too much vigor.

I learned that when brushing with an inky material, said inky material may fly over the walls, the mirror, the sink and the countertop.

In the mirror, I saw black teeth, a black tongue and black lips, and of course, beautiful silvery white hair. I looked like a strange guest at one of Truman Capote's Black and White Balls.

I brushed and brushed, and the black finally came off my teeth.

This might be the secret of the activated charcoal. Is it possible your teeth are so tarred with the charcoal that you brush and brush like you've never brushed before, resulting in the cleanest teeth of your life?

White hair, black teeth, not exactly progress. I'll spare you the details of my efforts to use a sunless tanner this summer. My legs are so blindingly white that small children shun their faces when they see me in my Capris and summer sandals.

Fall and cooler weather are here, and I'll wear a hat, long pants, and keep my mouth shut.

CHAPTER THIRTY-FIVE

Performance Art for the Mature Woman

Going to the Museum of Modern Art in New York is on my list of "Top Ten Favorite Activities." MoMA houses my favorite painting *Starry Night* along with some memorable works by Matisse and Wyeth's *Christina's World*. The latter has taken my breath away since I first saw it reprinted in a fifth-grade art book.

But MoMA has new "art" in the way of performance art from Oscar-winning actress Tilda Swinton. She is best known in America as the British actress who won the 2007 Best Supporting Actress for *Michael Clayton*.

Her performance art, called *The Maybe*, features the blonde actress sleeping in a glass box. The Twitterverse, and others I don't care about, praised her performance.

For those of us who are not long, lanky, lean, leggy and luscious, I will share "Performance Art for the Mature Woman," baby boomer-style. The audience is allowed in at this time, or they may wait for the movie version, entitled "The Bed and the Bedraggled."

To prepare for the performance art:

Step A:

1. Use the bathroom. Get all the stuff out on the bathroom counter that you need to prepare.

2. Put hair up in blue nylon headband. Remove make-up with Olay Regenerist Moist Towelette and apply mass quantities of cold cream-like substance. Brush teeth with Walgreens battery-powered toothbrush while singing the ear-worm you can't get out of your head, *"Patches, I'm depending on you, son"* and enjoy the vibrato that results. Now floss your

teeth after digging through three or four drawers to find the floss. Now wash your face with warm water and throw the now dirty washcloth in the bathtub with a fling (that's part of the art.)

3.   Remove your clothing and put on one of your dead mother's nightgowns that you could not bear to throw away a year ago when she died. Take off your socks and look through your four sock drawers until you find the specially-infused aloe socks that are covered with tiny pink peace symbols. Put them on.

4. Use the bathroom.

Step B:

1. Use the bathroom again.

2. Find the bottle of melatonin and take one.

Step C:

1. Prepare the bed.

2. Find your Nook, Nook cord, laptop, cell phone, current puzzle book, emery board, reading glasses, sleeping glasses (the old pair you wear to sleep in so you can see when you get up to go to the bathroom), extra blanket, recent issue of *Time* magazine, a journal, blue Sharpie, yellow highlighter, red ink pen, black fountain pen, Foot Joy catalog, L.L. Bean catalog, Great Courses catalog, and last Sunday's *New York Times* and put all of them in the center of the bed, north of the husband, east of the cat.

3. Get your eye-drops and put them on the side table next to the bed.

4. Use the bathroom.

5. Go to the kitchen and get a big glass of ice water from the fridge and put next to your bed.

6. Remember that you forgot to get two Clementines and go back to the kitchen and get the Clementines and two paper napkins, which you should place in the center of the bed. Eat the Clementines; keep the paper towel.

Step C:

1. Prepare the "Pillow System."

2. Pick up all the pillows that your husband and the cat have thrown on the floor, including the three bed pillows, two red round fuzzy pillows, the blue DogBone pillow, and the one that looks like a cylinder you draw in geometry class.

3. Place all the pillows in the order you must have to sleep.

4. Use the bathroom once again.

Step D:

1. Get into bed by carefully adjusting the cat, pillows, and all your crap in the middle of the bed, pushing most of it to the side where your husband is snoring. Use your eye-drops and spill them all over yourself and the cat, who is not amused.

2. Make a silly little hat for the cat out of the paper towel you used when you ate the Clementines. Make a game of putting the hat on the cat and when he knocks it off, put it back on.

3. When the cat is bored with the hat game, get up and go to the bathroom and throw the hat away. Use the bathroom. Return to the bed and get a sock from one of your four sock drawers (preferably the one full of socks with no mates). Put the sock on the cat's head to make him look like one of those elderly ladies in a Rembrandt painting. Do this several times until the cat is bored.

4. Now that your husband is good and asleep, turn on the bedroom light and start writing in your journal with a

scratchy fountain pen making as much noise as possible. Realize that your idea is so good, so compelling, so full of life and heart and promise that you have to get up immediately and go to your office and type it on the computer. This ticks the cat off who walks down his kitty stairs (Kitty is so old, he has a little set of stairs just to get on the bed) and stands at the office door meowing. This wakes the husband up. (The audience really likes this part.)

5. The husband mumbles something like, *"Can't you sleep like a normal person?"* The answer to that is, *"No."* But, you return to bed, turn off the bedroom light, and turn on the television with the mute button on, and watch four episodes of *House Hunters*.

6. Before finally going to sleep, use the bathroom. Yet, again.

Isn't this much more entertaining than the actress at MoMA?

ABOUT THE AUTHOR

Amy McVay Abbott is a freelance writer, hailing from the Hoosier state.

This book is a compilation of columns published in Indiana newspapers in Alexandria, Crawfordsville, Columbia City, Connersville, Elwood, Evansville, Logansport, Plymouth, Tipton and Washington between 2009 and 2013. Some of these essays also appeared on *Open Salon*, *Red Room*, and *The Broad Side*.

Abbott's work has been featured in *Salon*, *Our USA*, *Alter-net*, *Talking Writing*, *Fictionique*, *Erma Bombeck Writer's Workshop Blog*, *Does This Make Sense*, *Mamapedia*, as well as local and regional magazines. She has a bachelor's and a master's degree in journalism from Ball State University.

She is also the author of *The Luxury of Daydreams* (WestBow Press, 2011), available through the usual book sites.

You can find Amy McVay Abbott on-line at www.amyabbottwrites.com. Watch for *A Piece of Her Heart* in 2014.

If you like this book, consider posting a review on Amazon or Goodreads or your own blog or favorite social media site.

ACKNOWLEDGEMENTS

Special thanks to my husband, Randy (sometimes called as Herman in my work) for his ongoing support as a proofreader, editor, spelling and fact checker, and the source for much material. He is the funniest person I ever knew.

Special thanks to Diana Ani Stokely for her cover design and technical support, and to Ruth Stanley, for her editorial guidance. Ruth, I'm sorry we disagree about the spelling of the word "acknowledgements or acknowledgments."

The Luxury of Daydreams (2011)

Also available at amazon.com

Fort Wayne Arts Magazine, Whatzsup, Evan Gillespie

There's a quietness to living in Indiana that some Hoosiers detest. Having lived here my entire life, I can say with some acquired authority that it takes a certain kind of resolution to be satisfied with staying here in the Midwest, especially the part of the Midwest that's removed from a large urban area, and over the years I've struggled to keep that resolution in place. It comes and it goes; some days this place is unbearably tedious and lacking, and some days it seems like the perfect place to be. I suspect that Amy McVay Abbott has those ups and downs too, but in *The Luxury of Daydreams*, a collection of personal essays, she effectively captures mostly the good days, those days during which this kind of life seems more than adequate.

Abbott's book is the appealing kind of essay collection in which a writer's life comes into view gradually, gaining focus with each piece of the puzzle that falls into place, revealing a picture little by little, slowly rather than all at once. Her story isn't uncovered chronologically, and it almost seems unfair to summarize her biography in a straightforward way here. I'll do it, though. She grew up in Whitley County, went to college at Ball State University, worked as a journalist, moved to Florida for a bit, got married and had a child, returned to southern Indiana and reclaimed her life as a Hoosier. She writes about each of these experiences and how they shaped the woman she is today. There are themes that run throughout *The Luxury of*

Daydreams, and they are the essential values of the Midwest, the kinds of values that everyone thinks of when they think of the virtues of the Heartland. Family, history, faith, compassion, self-sufficiency, a respect for the land.

You couldn't write a more concise textbook with which to teach someone about the things that characterize the better parts of the Midwest than Abbott has written here, and the book doesn't do much to shake up any preconceived notions an outsider might have about this place. That's not to say it's all smooth sailing and small town quaintness. There is struggle and difficulty here, too. The whole impetus to write the book begins when Abbott loses her job, but what is the Midwest about these days if not unemployment?

She deals with personal challenges (her son has Asperger's Syndrome, and her mother suffers from dementia) and she helps other people cope with their own tragedies (she loses a good friend to leukemia, and she does what she can to be supportive to the woman's family). But Abbott gets over these hurdles with the help of Christian faith and an impressive stockpile of old fashioned Midwestern resilience. There's never any doubt whether she'll be all right in the end. Part of what helps her keep looking ahead with optimism is her ability to look backward with clarity.

She learns about – and teaches us about – her ancestors, Indiana farmers who never wanted to be anything other than what they were, men and women who stood up to the vagaries of nature and the economy, untimely death and every other hardship that came their way with steadfastness. Abbott treasures the objects they passed down to her – a quilt, a mixing bowl, a photograph – as a means to remember where she came from and as an example of how she should keep going. She writes all of this in a manner that's evocative and engaging. The best Midwestern writers can find poetry in what looks mundane to the unimaginative, and Abbott occupies a space firmly within that tradition. It's not always easy to look around Indiana and see what Abbott sees, but it's good to be reminded that all the good that she finds in this place is here if you're willing to notice it. October 6, 2011 On Books EVAN GILLESPIE

WHAT I LEARNED FROM MY HOOSIER FRIEND AMY, Review by Richard Brown, author of *Send in the Clown Car: Race for the White House 2012*

I knew I would enjoy her first book, *The Luxury of Daydreams*, and I did. There's the chapter on the birth of her child ("Childbirth itself is a gruesome affair where the guest of honor is woefully indifferent to the hostess"), a child she now describes as "the young man who lives in our basement three months a year." (Been there, done that.) There's her embarrassing adventure as an unprepared Bingo caller ("Cut out the jokes, and move on, girlie-girl"), as well as the embarrassment of a father who remembers all your mistakes ("Do you remember my daughter and how much ice cream she ate at Guernsey Field Day?").

What I didn't expect was how much her book made me think. No, it's not a collection of opinion pieces. Rather, the book is a series of reminiscences about growing up and living in the heart of the Heartland in Indiana. When a good writer evokes her life vividly, as Amy has, it's only natural for the reader to compare hers to his own life.

Amy is several years younger than I am, but she and I both grew up in smaller sized towns in the early 1960s. Her prose reminds me of a time when I could ride my bicycle all over town without fear and without wearing armor like Sir

Lancelot. It reminds me of a time when kids ran out to play with the neighbors' kids and parents didn't have to obsess about their whereabouts, because neighbors watched out for each other. It reminds me of a time when generations lived in the same town, and daughters married in the same churches their mothers did. It also reminds me of a time, however, when those churches usually inspired compassion, not condemnation. It reminds me of a time when small towns provided sufficient jobs for its residents.

That life seems to be fading away. When I was a kid, I used to play touch football on our street, a street that is now overrun by parked cars and hulking SUVs. The neighborhood kids and I used to play pick-up baseball games in summers on the high school field, a field now fenced in and accessible only for approved, organized activities. Today I don't even know the names of many of my neighbors.

The big difference between our lives is revealed in a chapter entitled "Sweatshirt Weather," in which Amy writes, "Harvest is in full swing in October, if not finished. Beans and corn are picked; winter wheat is planted." In the town where I grew up, the only place you'll find beans and corn is in the produce section of the supermarket. There are no farmers here. My town is a bedroom community for Manhattan commuters; it's the home of Don Draper in *Mad Men*.

I find myself jealous of Amy's ties to the land and the seasons. I wonder if our disconnection from them is a contributing factor to why so many of us feel adrift in our lives.

Our ancestors worked to live. They had no time for angst. They tilled the soil to prevent starvation; they built homes to provide shelter; they knitted clothes to keep warm.

Now it takes so few people to create our basic needs of life that many of us engage in careers that may be considered inessential.

I've always wondered what Thomas Jefferson would think were he to somehow appear in 21st-century America. If he saw everyone walking around with their attention drawn to the electronic devices in their hands, would he admire our technological advances or be alarmed at our isolation from our neighbor? If he saw young men being paid millions of dollars to play a game, and other men paid hundreds of thousands just to comment on those games, or people becoming rich and famous merely for allowing reality-TV cameras in their homes, would he applaud our independence from the struggle to survive or would he be dismayed at our eager embrace of so much shallowness?

Though I've been a lifelong suburbanite, I felt the pull of rural living for one week each summer when my family would pack into our car and drive seven hours north to spend a week with my Aunt Mildred in Vermont. Mildred and her husband John owned 120 acres of land outside the state capitol of Montpelier, up a long hill on a dirt road. From her front porch, you couldn't see another house, and a passing car was an event. The land across the dirt road, part of her property, was wild, the grass often too tall to walk in. The appearance of a deer at the dining room window was a common occurrence.

There was enough land in front of the house for me and my brothers to play wiffle ball daily. The front porch of the house was the right field fence, while the wooden deer at the other end of the driveway served as the left field fence. It felt strange and exotic at night to turn on my transistor radio and hear Red Sox, not Yankee, games. (Mildred's daughter

Alice, bless her heart, spent the last month of her life driving around Florida watching spring training.)

Amy's chapter on working as a carhop at a restaurant that featured root beer floats reminded me that, when we were in Vermont, we'd occasionally spend an evening at the A & W root beer stand. I Googled it; it's no longer there.

I never visited Mildred's home again once I left for college. She died two decades ago, predeceased by her husband, and Alice soon followed. The property was sold.

A few years ago, we were vacationing in another part of Vermont with the kids, and I decided to take a drive past Mildred's house. I didn't need directions to find my way, and soon enough I was on that long, hilly road, still gloriously unpaved. All of the old landmarks were still there, and for a moment, I started to feel like that 14-year-old kid anxious to grab his Wiffle ball bat.

As we neared Mildred's old house, however, my heart sank. Every inch of her property had been developed. The wild land across the dirt road now consisted of manicured lawns and long driveways leading to brand, spanking-new McMansions. I couldn't even see Mildred's old house to see if it had been remodeled; the old home plate of my wiffle ball field was now part of a line of trees along the road that hid the house from view.

I'm sure the families that owned the new homes were thrilled. The neighborhood was green, safe and secure, a nice place to raise a family. But I was thoroughly disheartened by how rapidly "progress" had buried any trace of Mildred's existence, as if the half-century she had spent on that quiet land had never happened.

In Amy Abbott's world, the past still has value and community is real, not virtual. *The Luxury of Daydreams* brought these memories, good and bad, rushing back to me. Her direct declarative sentences gave her pieces an added punch. I wish we had more Amys in our world, but I also wish we had more of her world in our world.

REVIEW by LC Neal

LC Neal is the founder and Editor-in-Chief of <u>Fictionique</u>, a literary ezine catering to fiction writers, essayists, artists and poets. She is also a fiction writer herself, with one novel nearly completed and a second in its infancy. She occasionally wanders off course and reviews music, books and television. She has a deep and lifelong attachment to historical research, which simply refuses to resolve itself into any sort of profitable enterprise.

Coming from a long line of terminally skeptical smart asses, when someone hands me a book entitled *The Luxury of Daydreams* and follows it up with "it's kind of spiritual," my first response is: I should not be reading this book. Much less reviewing it. I have a reputation to maintain.

I fully expected to struggle mightily with arriving at what to say about this collection of deeply personal essays, and surprised myself by struggling, all right - struggling to figure out why the emotion evoked by this book was so comforting. That feeling drove me crazy for a couple of days, until my much reduced memory banks finally sputtered and spat out the thing I had been reaching for.

I was homesick.

Because there is heartbreak and struggle and loss and tragedy in McVay Abbott's world and throughout her family's history. But it's offset, by far more generous doses of what the lucky among us associate with home: comfort, humor, family, tradition, love and hope.

About hope: unable to live in a world without it, the author does what we all should and finds it, in the smallest and largest ways. McVay Abbott's essay on the subject is one of my favorites....as she puts it, members of her family are Cubs fans, for heaven's sake. What's more hopeful than that?

The circumstances described in her tales are not exclusive to her by any means, but McVay Abbott's way of balancing the good and the bad is unique. She finds room to laugh when many wouldn't, and time to cry without an ounce of self-pity when she must, and always, always keeps her eye on her particular prize: her husband, her son, her family, her friends, her faith. She is firmly rooted in the same soil her ancestors were, and her obvious admiration for what it took her predecessors to build the foundation that her family rests on is woven through everything she writes.

The best thing of all about *The Luxury of Daydreams* is its structure. It's a small book, but big enough to hold a piece of all of us, contained therein. You'll recognize yourself....and your best friend. Probably a family member or two. But mostly you'll recognize Amy McVay Abbott, as that sister who cracks you up at the most formal occasions, that friend who flies to your defense whether you need it or not, the woman who calls bingo for a bunch of cranky seniors who don't get her jokes.

She's the person who keeps all those separate pieces of humanity that make a family close to each other, and to her own heart.

REVIEW by Vanessa Seijo

Vanessa Seijo is a writer/teacher living in Puerto Rico. She is currently working on an YA adventure series.

She is the author of <u>Nicolás, la abuela Margot y el hechicero,</u> Ediciones SM 2010, Puerto Rico.

Journalist Amy McVay Abbott's debut book, *The Luxury of Daydreams*, WestBow Press 2011, is a fantastic collection of essays, reflections of a life well-lived with the promise of more to come.

The Luxury of Daydreams is an aptly titled book that will speak to all of us. It touches upon the very fabric of our lives, what we believe and what we think we believe, our families, our loves, our losses. It is the kind of book that reminds you that it is never too late to set out to do what you intended to do; but, it also helps you honor the sacrifices made along the way, accepting life as less than perfect, still wonderful in its very essence. It reminds you of what is important.

The first chapter is a brilliant choice. Those first pages still the mind and prepare the reader for a soulful adventure. McVay Abbott is an engaged writer, both with her beliefs and with her readers.

There are essays that are true snapshots of a time gone by, slices of delightful Americana as well as faithful portraits of difficult times; all survived with hard work, faith, and optimism. McVay Abbott's description of autumn brings a lovely ache of something sorely missed. There are turns of phrase that will make you laugh out loud even as the very words quietly show you a truth so profound you will find your eyes have traitorously filled with silent tears. Words that reflect life's mysteries, as simple as they are deep.

147

The essays on growing up and friendship are sweet and poignant, but not rosy colored. They are brutally honest while still being gorgeously composed. This is a writer who is not afraid to question herself.

Through it all, McVay Abbott's delightful comedic sense will delight you. There are the amusing stories of motherhood. The bingo story will rightly have you in stitches. You will fall in love with a wild grandmother who carries reptiles in a picnic basket. And in this book you will finally find out just who the "Mayor of Dorkytown" really is.

The Luxury of Daydreams is the kind of book that becomes a conversation between author and reader. You will find yourself stopping mid-sentence and saying out loud "Amy, about that bit, you know it reminds me" and realize you are, sadly, not in front of the writer sharing a cup of coffee under a shaded tree in your patio. But you will wish, more than once, that she were there right next to you.

For this book is a journey of self discovery in which you might also learn a lot about yourself. Whether you are a believer or not, this is one book not to be missed.

REVIEW by Mathew Paust, author of *Sacrifice*, *Executive Pink*, and *If the Woodsman is Late*.

I lost sleep reading *The Luxury of Daydreams*. I do most of my recreational reading at night, in bed, to supplant whatever frets and fusses of the day might be lingering to obstruct an easy slide into raveled sleeve of care-knitting sleep. My readings also occasionally inspire my subconscious mind with ideas for pillow dreams. *The Luxury of Daydreams* did the latter, sparking, and mingling with mine, memories of Christmas mornings, personal embarrassments, family gatherings, sibling wars, old friends, loss, dreams within dreams, small town magic and a moment that stole the joy from Three Dog Night in a mostly friendlier time less complicated and politically portentous, it seemed, than the present.

Perhaps Amy's stories resonated so deeply within me because I grew up in a small Midwestern town, too, and so many of the people and experiences she describes could, and do, reside in my memory, albeit with different names.

I have only two bones to pick with Amy as I read her spellbinding stories, hoping they would ease me into my own dreamland. First, her writing is so artful and fascinating I had a tough time returning the book to my nightstand and putting out the light. Second, hackles pricked up on my neck at her mention of her hometown as "America's best small town," because my hometown is the best—or at least it was back then. I was tempted to snarl and hurl her book across the bedroom, but then it occurred to me that in our memories the towns in which Amy and I grew up—hers in Indiana, mine in Wisconsin - were virtually the same.

If you wish to read the most revealing and comprehensive story in this collection first, I suggest "Letter to my Seventeen-Year-Old Self." Read this before the others, this flash review of her coming-of-age through the eyes of her older, wiser accomplished self and you will catch an indelible glimpse of Amy as a fun-loving sister, a mischievous daughter and a warm, generous, happy-hearted friend.

Made in the USA
San Bernardino, CA
06 December 2013